CHINA IS NEAR

Marco Bellocchio

CHINA IS NEAR

With an introduction by Tommaso Chiaretti

Translated from the Italian by Judith Green

The Orion Press · New York

Contents

CHINA IS NEAR

Allegretto Con Pessimismo

by Tommaso Chiaretti

China. Geographical region, nation, political regime, culture, tradition, rice, wall, cultural revolution, Mao, ideograms, danger, hope. China is an abstraction, a chain of abstractions. To say "China is near" is to turn an abstraction into the pivot of a metaphor. What is it that really is, or ought to be, "near" us? That is, what are the concrete specifics of the idea of "China" as it appears in the newspapers we read, in the posters we see in the streets, in the images transmitted to us on television? What is China today? What does it represent for a peaceable bourgeois, for an integrated proletarian, for a student rebelling against school and family, for a young film director, for a housewife? What actually is that much-discussed, puzzling, contradictory movement which upsets exhausted terminology and defines itself "cultural revolution"? Is this a bad translation or an ugly habit? Why do the "Red Guards" want to burn Shakespeare? And what does Shakespeare represent for a young Chinese barely arrived from the fields? Why do conceptions which are objectively laughable and unquestionably uncouth to the ears of Westerners well-educated in the technique and dimension of the art film arouse not only the attention but also the ostentatious adherence of responsible intellectuals? Why has the "China" phenomenon such lively resonance among political and cultural protest groups on the left: minorities within minorities, dominated by the young, provincial in a non-limiting sense? Why did Godard call his last film *La Chinoise*? And is Bellocchio simply a sensitive author culling the tension of a culturally and politically natural phenomenon? Or is he inside that phenomenon, participating in it with suffering and impatience?

A host of questions like these arose even before the film *China Is Near* was made, following the provocative announcement that an Italian director who had barely made his debut was now going to make a "political" film and this is what he was going to call it. It was known for certain, from the biographies, that Bellocchio is involved on the fringes of a minoritarian political faction. It was supposed that certain of his attitudes are born in the environment of a small journal like *Quaderni Piacentini* (the *Piacenza Notebooks*), which is edited, furthermore, by one of Bellocchio's brothers. From here it was easy to jump to journalistic conclusions: we were about to see the cinematic "manifesto" of the "Chinese" groups in Italy. Hence the whole series of uninformed misunderstandings.

But at the first contact with the film it becomes obvious that it's quite another kettle of fish. *China Is Near* does present itself as a *political* film, and this certainly makes its citizenship in the Italian motion picture industry rather awkward. But it is a political film only in that "politics" is its theme, its evident justification. This is a film born of a judgment (never expressed explicitly and yet always before us) on Italian society and its progressive weakening, but it proposes no solution; and it negates in its facts and in its characters the possibility of any real effective intervention by groups that move in an environment in which only "contestation" and protest are feasible. Its political character, that is, lies in its placing itself outside professional politics, in its desire to demolish this myth, in its ironic reflection on politics as a method or expedient of liberation from individual and social complexes.

What is more, the novelty in this sort of focus is the fact that the polemic is not directed against diametrically opposed objectives, against macroscopic corruption, against an enemy declared and discovered. On the contrary, the target is limited here to a range of variations which often escape the superficial newspaper reader who thinks all cats are gray. Bellocchio obviously moves in an environment where subjects like permanent revolution, class consciousness, and third world are discussed without hesitation. And his skepticism about the way those entangled in the bourgeois rules of the game are supposed to impede the continuation of a revolutionary development with their illusions of reformers in spite of themselves, [1] has an advantage over other analogous positions, for it is not at all disturbed by the resentments and repressed wrath of the *ex's*—those who had sworn too much and now have taken up an ardent campaign of methodical doubt and rejection of party diplomacy. Bellocchio's position is prejudiced by neither the dramatic break with Stalinistic subjugation in politics nor the rejection of socialist realism in art. He has reached an avant-garde position (if it may be called such) by other paths, perhaps more sincere, more sure and less seminated with mental reservations. No mortgages or excommunications shadow his legitimate idea that the only possible road to a revolutionary solution must necessarily pass through the rejection of all integrationary tactics.

Every one of Bellocchio's characters goes through an identical process, though in different ways. Each one, more or less self-consciously, seeks (or in any case finds) maximum integration in the social structure—which Bellocchio, without moralizing, considers the renunciation of their ideals. This itinerary is spasmodic for all the characters, not only for the protagonist Vittorio, whose exhibitionism and urbane laicism are so obvious. Carlo, the bookkeeper, is fed up with holding the stirrup for a horse that doesn't run, and wants at least to get up in the saddle. Giovanna, the secretary, wants the game to be carried through; she had perhaps had the momentary illusion, in the blasphemous love-making under the portraits of the fathers of Socialism, of believing in women's emancipation, but she finds herself instead back in all the commonplace conceptions of the provincial girl. And Elena, who is the most firmly set on the pedestal of class, finds herself beaten by the aggression of the Socialist social-climber, who though apparently coarse is a good

1. The reference is to the Italian Communist Party, thought to have been tamed by excessive concessions to the democratic process.

seducer. But even Camillo, the young "Chinese," ends up in the same inevitable situation. Vittorio has characterized his itinerary to perfection: "You can be Marxist-Leninist but still insist that your sister doesn't screw around."

It might be paradoxically deduced, with a plentiful arsenal of arguments taken from this context, that Vittorio's judgment of the situation in general as well as of Camillo in particular is the most pertinent and accurate of the political judgments explicit or implicit here, and that his cynical analysis is the most fitting, even if ideologically incorrect: "The things you believe in, and which in the last analysis I believe in too, will never be accomplished now. To think something's just, but not to believe it can be accomplished, means one doesn't even believe it's just." This is an old argument that is repeated by many today in terms not very different from these, and certainly not less pharisaical.

Even the Socialist candidate's final speech seems to be based on a model from reality, and leads us to think that he is giving us (though in a ridiculous form) the *reality* of the Center-Left government coalition and not just its rhetorical justification: a constant generic reference to Progress and an explicit refusal to refer to Karl Marx. The revolutionary moment is considered as a sort of sentimental paradigm, a necessary experience of adolescents to be forgotten in the process of developing an existence of compromise. An earlier speech of Vittorio's—"we're already dead"—is the other, less haughty, side of the same confession or analysis: a socialism which declares its own *rigor mortis* in confronting the question of social structure, and then refuses to consider problems in which ideology and "principles" —like international questions and the great choices—tend to become overly involved. All is reduced to small and ambiguous casuistry within the solid mold of the provincial microcosm.

Is there another possibility—a proposition which, although not explicit, can be perceived between the lines of the film? If we accept as a given fact (to which it has not even been thought necessary to refer in *China Is Near*) a judgment on the equivocal position and social-democratization of the Communist Party in

Italy, then there is still another road left: total revolt in the name of principle. But a revolt which does not take the forms—inconclusive and vain—of the exploits of Camillo. Such protest, if identified with the presumptuous aspirations of this boy (a natural son of his class, although apparently rebelling against it) immediately becomes a part or a move in the game: opposition as generous and sincere as you like, but in substance fictitious, futile and not even as scandalous as it would like to think itself. There's a bomb which raises a great cloud of smoke; there's a reliquary and a Catholic school and a uniform one hasn't the courage to soil. There's a flood of domestic lies ("In my heart I couldn't think why she shouldn't still be a virgin"), and a sign on a wall and an argument with a poor night-watchman. Nothing more: the portrait of Lenin and the mad recital of stereotyped formulas are the descriptive elements of this fetishistic phase, of this sour impotence which is made explicit in the transparent allegory of Camillo's sexual inexperience at the beginning of the film.

This is not the place to discuss whether this analysis is correct or incomplete, partial or partisan. And we should also have to go back to certain theories about partisanship in art which there's no point in exhuming here, resisting the temptation to turn them against those who have sustained them clumsily and vexaciously. Nevertheless, it can already be established whether or not these characters are significant in the current reality of Italian politics, even without getting into the debate over the meaning of "typical." The image of the ardent interparty, interclass, interreligious ecumenical embrace is unquestionably relevant, even if it may upset the exulting ranks of the intellectuals who were so moved and excited by the recent birth of the new Unified Socialist Party here, on the model of the English Labour Party.

It is worthy of note that all this comes from an author whose background is rather particular. We cannot be surprised by the fact that he is young: he has not posed as a prodigal child, bringing up to date the themes, modes and interests of other generations of film-makers; he has not adapted Thomas Mann or Moravia; he has not got the experience of anti-Fascism, the

Resistance or the elections of 1948 behind him. He extracts things and attitudes from himself and from his own generation. He rediscovers buried and abandoned loves with the eyes of his age, the eyes of a young provincial intellectual of the left. He abounds in quotations, but not for the sake of metaphor. His Verdi has an absolutely opposite function from Visconti's. For him, melodrama is ridiculous—or worse, a sort of bourgeois consumer good—and he uses it to underline the impotence, the obtuseness and the physical ataxia of a class (Vittorio's *Don Carlos* in the bathtub, or *La Traviata* used in *Fists in the Pocket* with a mad and acuitous Wagnerian-Nietzschean significance). Donizetti is ridiculous for Bellocchio, and there's no disputing his declaration of shocking taste; we need only accept the fact that he has built one of the most irresistible sequences in his film on this idea. His literary citations are all in a farcical tone. Giacosa[1] and Shakespeare appear as if to force various characters into exhibitionism: the old aunts or the young "Chinese" in the confessional. Sometimes Bellocchio quotes even without being aware of it, in echoes or images of the provincial world caught in famous scenes; for example, Vittorio's resemblance to Gozzano's[2] Totò Merumeni: "twenty-five years, of temper scornful, / much culture and taste in rhymes, / scarce brains, scarce morals, and frightful / clair-voyance: the child of our times." Like Totò, "slow and supine," Vittorio possesses the girl of the inferior class "while the house sleeps." In the end, he seems to be a "socialist" in the same humanitarian and detached way that one "sends money to the poor," and tries in all honesty to convince the pious aunts that the Pope is further left than the Communists.

So we have a Gozzanian strain in Bellocchio, of which there was some suspicion in *Fists in the Pocket* too, in the sense of "pessimism without sadness" which Amalia Guglielmetti attributed to the

1. Giuseppe Giacosa (1847-1906), novelist and dramatist whose works are notoriously sentimental and moralistic.
2. Guido Gozzano (1883-1916), poet of the "Crepuscolari" or "Twilight" group (1903-1912), which specialized in a rosy-gray, sentimental but realistic portraiture of the Italian provincial world.

poet. Bellocchio's analyses, his harrowing observations of a world to which he does not feel alien, are unquestionably those of a pessimist. But here we have a courageous gaiety at the end, as in *Fists in the Pocket*: scandalous mockery, delight (never masochistic) in making faces, in verbal and iconographic atrocities which might even be accused of being sadistic. But if the intellectual and formal use of the sadistic repertory is standard operating procedure in all the fashionable intelligentsia, Bellocchio does not seem to fit the pattern. The series of deaths of the characters in his first film does not belong to the world of the Charenton asylum, Ale's epilepsy has no analogy in the torture of Prince Constant, and Bellocchio's attention to sex has no parallel in the refined exercises of Klossowsky. It all belongs, if anything, to the technique of voluntary humor, on the lines of certain of Stevenson's gags, or Dürrenmatt's—to the liberating process of wit as suggested by Freud. And then, at the very end of *China Is Near*, there is nothing particularly atrocious, nothing clinical. Where we might have expected cruelty of emphasis, the commentary is explicitly demystifying: the abortion episode is dominated by "Catholic education"; the massacre of sparrows is pitiless, taken as an element of methodical cruelty with the same intentions as the hunt at the beginning of Jean Renoir's *The Rules of the Game*.

The tone, the commentary, the twists and turns of the narrative are all, that is, unequivocally satirical. The grotesque that was already present (and not only implicitly) in *Fists in the Pocket* explodes here, where the only obstacle resisting it has been removed: that of the "pathological case." Aside from the facetious episode, à la Krafft-Ebing, of the girl overcome by hyperesthesia, everything is normal here. The old mansion hides no horrors in its dark corners—just nocturnal lovers looking for the door, just domestic odors of soup and crumpled sheets, of dogs and dust. The province is portrayed in what should be its most uproarious and most eccentric moment, the election campaign, but the reality is anything but exciting. The note of distrust in the electoral campaign—that is, in everything pompously denominated "democratic system of self-government"—is sounded from the very beginning. And subsequently, in the same key, the newspaper in the school toilet (an explicit symbol), the speech in the "Stalinist citadel" (where we see that even a term loaded with dark satrapic reminiscences may be expended gaily enough, with the sense of measure and proportion of a tavern brawl), the whole episode of the bomb in the Socialist Party headquarters (with that unexpected intervention of the obtuse and fumbling friar who joins the buffoon's gallery of Italian priests that Bellocchio has been assembling), and finally, the last speech —that squalid moment of vanity and of irresistible truthfulness— before a mute audience. Even the protest of the "Chinese" is here a sort of practical joke in a small-town dimension, a family feud: an elderly miser being dogged by mischievous children.

In Italy, the "political" cinema has been confined to two parallel and unpromising roads. On the one hand, the path of demagogic emphasis, the so-called "civil *engagement*"; on the other, the notorious phenomenon of *qualunquismo*.[1] Bellocchio is alien to the lessons of civism, as he has clearly demonstrated. In the last analysis, Vittorio himself might be the true teacher of this moralistic reformism: elected, he would certainly do his best to carry out his exiguous program. Vittorio, sitting in a movie theater, would applaud with sincere emotion a work on, say, building speculation—a document proving the necessity of a Center-Left government on the Scandinavian or English model. On the other hand is the attitude of the *uomo qualunque*, the man in the street, who feels oppressed by the professional politicians and finds no solution other than verbal agression against the politician as such, be he deputy, city councilman or party secretary. But the *qualunquista*, who reads the repeated denunciations of "partyocracy" in the great Milanese daily *Il Corriere della Sera*, is perfectly integrated in the system; he serves it in his daily grumbling, which acts as a safety valve for the weighty

1. From the political party *L'Uomo Qualunque*, the Common Man, which obtained a certain success in the period immediately following World War II with its semi-Fascist antagonism toward the democratic political process (the "party-ocracy" or domination of public life by partisan political organizations) as such.

democratic machine. His salvation is always the *status quo ante*, and for him there is always an *ante* better than any *post* that the loudspeaker can promise him. Bellocchio is not afflicted with this type of weakness, and obviously his Italy—though explicitly provincial and almost vernacular—is not the theater of the contests between Don Camillo and Peppone. The very dispute between the brothers in this film is in fact only a sham. It is suggested that both are circling around a false problem, and that if there is a final embrace, it will be in the name of politics —that is, of class—and not against it.

Bellocchio's point of departure is a thesis (or postulate, since his film does not furnish demonstrations) : the idea of a revolution that has not been made and will not be made until the left sheds its inferiority complex—that is, the feverish vocation to divisible power—and until it finds weapons other than isolated squads of back-page terrorists. But it is nevertheless true that this last desolate fringe is where the author's anxiety tries to move. He does not participate in the mystical messianic expectation of a natural explosion of class-consciousness in the working class: more than "pathetically present," this class is brutally and realistically absent in his film. But if we had to pick out a character who reveals some possibility of liberation, it would be Rospo, in his surly contestation from inside another nested box, in his greater consciousness of the existence of a less private perspective, and also in his proletarian physicalness. He is an *outsider* who will probably not develop openly, due to his sacrosanct distance for the *positive*.

It would not be difficult to balance out the accounts by closing the circle on this character, the only one who is not completely victimized by the heavy satire of the facts. But this would bring the discussion around again to Bellocchio's political ideas instead of his film : to the correctness of his political interpretation and not to the more general hypothesis he presents on contemporary Italy, to the way it is expounded in the story, the characters and the language of the film. *China Is Near* cannot be discussed as the manifesto of a faction or a group; no film can. Although there is a considerable temptation to evaluate the film on this ground, it must be emphasized that the film must be read in another, not contradictory, manner. The rational intention of the author was to create a work which would contest the widespread techniques of immobility and compromise and the integrationalist vocation of the Italian intellectual and politician. But the result is a sort of star-chamber proceeding, and only through a series of concentric broadening operations can we discover in it and in its particular narrative modes the propositions useful for that political, social and ideological debate suggested by the title.

China Is Near, that is to say, has the structure of a classical drama or comedy, and *mutatis mutandis*, it brings to mind the names of some great moralists of the theater, such as Ibsen and Schnitzler. The plot, for example, has a Nordic or Central European flavor. We are not at the Americans' point of visceral violence, nor at the interplay of abstractions. The characters are not bearers of philosophies: they have clear connotations of class or social level; imprisoned within their class, they sense its crisis and are subjected to aggression from without. The double mechanism of *déclassement* and *surclassement* takes shape with a plot structure out of a Parisian boulevard comedy, to the point where the parallel actions form into a symmetrical and geometrically exact pattern. We see two calculated actions—two seductions—weaving together into a suspenseful finale, resolved by a double wedding right out of a *pochade*. Except that matrimony and sex, for Bellocchio, for his little *Bel-Ami*, are means for climbing up one rank, not for "conquering" the lady's graces.

China, therefore, is anything but near. Here there's no talk of socialism and of revolution, of strikes and of more or less enlightened neocapitalism. Here we have palace intrigues as dingy as their protagonists. Who, after all, are not always silly, nor always base; they even have moments of chilling good-fellowship in their decision to climb together toward the modest summit.

For this narrative Bellocchio has imagined in the screenplay, and exalted in the parallel montage, a structure absolutely traditional in appearance. But there's tradition and tradition.

Bellocchio's tradition, in the cinema, is that of Buñuel—and this time the name, which already appeared in connection with *Fists in the Pocket,* can be invoked without seeming bizarre. The Buñuel of the chilling stories of bourgeois calculation, *The Diary of a Chambermaid,* where the entanglement of the villainous private pact and the political situation is another pit stuck in the craw of the "respectable."

There's an obvious congruity between *Fists in the Pocket* and *China Is Near* in their diabolical persistency in analyzing family relations—a characteristic Italo-Catholic-bourgeois taboo. The points of contact between the two films are more explicit than they seem. For example, the symptomatic recurrence of the religious education (the collection of edifying literature in the first film, and the Catholic children's *Il Vittorioso,* or *The Victorious,* in the amply described, more completely composed setting of the Catholic boarding-school). If there is a difference, it lies precisely in the narrative structure and in the language, which in the first film was broken, bitter, gasping, aggressive and explosive in its inconsistent associations, and now is more calculated, attentive, measured, rarely elliptical and almost always direct and explicit—in a word, captionlike. The spectator is no longer forced into a sort of logical synthesization to which he is unaccustomed; perhaps there is greater "respect" for the *consumer* and his weaknesses. In this sense some may wish to observe—favorably or unfavorably—that the author has completed an "adolescent" phase as a film-maker and is now facing more adult narrative problems, with a more lucid and non-anarchistic consciousness of the real situation; that is, of the so-called *market.*

The problem of how much a break with the normal language of the movie industry is *in itself* an eversion, and how much a system of traditional signs may be *in itself* an objective integration into the structure of that industry, clearly goes beyond the way in which *China Is Near* was conceived and produced. It can only be said that the film has all the characteristics of a *second work* of a young man tenaciously searching. It adds new stimuli, clarifies unanswered questions, and offers further possibilities for the identification of all the gifts of a true artist who has not exhausted himself in his first opus. Who clearly is not fond of reciting the role of "promising young talent" assigned to him by the condescension of teachers on whose words few can swear.

The Authors On Tape

Tape-recorded conversation among Tommaso Chiaretti, Marco Bellocchio and Elda Tattoli during the last phase of the making of the film.

CHIARETTI: Let's start with the title, which is the first element that offers polemical possibilities. As the film reaches the public it has to free itself of the burden of opinions and prejudices—pro and con—which it has collected along the way. It has often been supposed to be a story set among the "Chinese" of the Italian provinces, or even the manifesto of these tiny groups. Obviously the spectator will be able to see for himself just what's up. But since there are political themes in the film, and since you were fully conscious of what you were doing, we ought to start by asking your own opinion. That is, what is the meaning of the phrase "China is near" for you? And what does it mean for each of your protagonists?

BELLOCCHIO: The slogan I've taken for the title of the film *China Is Near* can be interpreted in at least two ways. Aside from my own personal desire that China be as near as possible (a desire which is obviously worthless on the critical as well as the practical level), I should say that, paradoxically, China is very distant for those who think it near, and very near for those who think it far away. For instance, if the behavior of Camillo (a false "Sinophile")—vain, presumptuous, egocentric, like an esthete of revolution—contradicts the menace and provocation in the title, the behavior of his older brother and sister, Vittorio and Elena—their extreme sentimental vulnerability, their morbid attachment to property (although in different ways), their total enslavement to the rules of the class they belong to—is a warning that there is a *China* not far from them, China in this case being a not-distant day of reckoning for a certain style of life: the crumbling, the annihilation of a decrepit and disintegrating form of life.

CHIARETTI: You say that Camillo is a *false Sinophile*, an esthete of revolution. This is clear. Then we wonder what is a *true Sinophile?* And why is it that these "true Sinophiles," or (leaving aside a formula which is fairly worn-out) these minority groups on the left do not appear in the film? You say that there is a *day of reckoning* in store for the bourgeoisie represented by Vittorio and Elena. Obviously this is a "reckoning" from inside their class, irreparable, which will occur without any revolutionary pressure. Now in reality Vittorio appears as something different from the representative of a bourgeoisie on the road towards disintegration. He is a social democrat who is fully conscious of the contemporary process of reinforcement of the bourgeoisie. And this process will make him win, for now, at least in the terms of the dialectic outlined in the film. In other words, if Camillo is impotent, and his friends as well, what can stop Vittorio from being elected, from participating in political power, from reinforcing it? Ridicule alone isn't enough.

BELLOCCHIO: This film is trying to exemplify two simple and precise convictions. First, that the process of social-democratic involution will go on for many years to come, without finding any real difficulties in its path. And second, that it's impossible to ally with those who oppose this social reality but continue to talk on the basis of a social-democratic platform. Since we believe that this state of affairs is anything but fragile and temporary, we wanted in this film at least to negate it, with all the dramatic means we were able to marshal for a result which would not only be damaging to the reactionaries properly speaking, but which would also, more specifically, be able to unmask (or at least to provoke and irritate) all those satirical authors of the

Italian cinema who feel themselves the caustic correctors of this social-democratic state of affairs but who in the end, with a helpless shrug, accept it.

CHIARETTI: I'll ask you the question more directly. Evidently, if you were able to conceive such a film, you not only had to have factual documentation; in a certain sense you didn't even have to look for it, for you already knew personally the position of the minority left in Italy and were an adherent of it. From this situation you developed your idea, or you were inspired by it. You started out saying that you yourself hope that China really is near. Then what is it, according to you, in the dislocation, in the ideology and in the strategy of the "Chinese" groups in Italy that prevents them from penetrating into or being heard by the working class, from modifying the strategy of the parties which with more or less sincerity call themselves "Marxist"? That is, the Communist Party and the Italian Socialist Party of Proletarian Unity.

BELLOCCHIO: The position of total opposition to neo-capitalist society has come to be called, correctly, "Chinese." In Italy, too, this "Chinese" opposition is growing in proportion to the increasingly compromising politics of the traditional workers' parties. There's no point in emphasizing here the political differences between China and the revolutionary struggles in Vietnam and South America on the one hand, and the Italian "Sinophile" movement on the other. Let me say here only that the Italian "Chinese" are as able in public demonstrations (which they often succeed in making extremistic, and where they show courage and decisiveness against great odds) as they are dogmatic and abstract on the theoretical side. The fact is that the aim of applying Maoist principles and strategy *sic et simpliciter* to Italy (and to all capitalistically advanced countries) is ingenuous. But what is important above all is that this total, *Chinese* opposition (which includes Marxist-Leninists, *provos*, certain Catholics, action groups and study groups) should develop in a way that either the workers' parties have to take it into account or else that it become an alternative movement, a real political force. This sort of analysis is widespread. I've found several very interesting examples in *Quaderni Piacentini*, for instance.

CHIARETTI: But your film is clearly satirical. And the very fact that you set the story in the provinces signifies a move toward a conventional type of provincial farce. Now, it's obvious that you didn't intend to use the techniques of a Germi, for instance, to satirize the political situation rather than matrimonial or sexual prejudices. And you didn't do it. But all the same there's an explosion of the ridiculous here—and very funny it is, too—which is made even more obvious by the weaknesses of the opposing forces in play here. What I mean is that if you had set it in Turin, for instance, instead of the small city of Imola, at the time of the Fiat strikes—the conflict among protest groups of the left and the police and the Communists and the employers—it would have called for a different descriptive approach.

BELLOCCHIO: The people in the film are, furthermore, *provincial Chinese*, and the projection of metropolitan phenomena into the provinces is always very much reduced and less fiery. The margin of action in the provinces is obviously much smaller (for numerical reasons above all, and also because certain types of conditioning, such as that of the family, are stronger) and the classic defects of the provinces—above all, verbalism—afflict even the "Chinese." The context and the general tone of caricature of the film cannot but attack the "Chinese" too.

CHIARETTI: I'd like to add something else too: that besides the provincial setting, the film deals with choices rather closely bound up with the family environment, more than with strictly political choices. And also that the problem of revolt and integration is fairly limited to this environment.

BELLOCCHIO: As far as the "Sinophiles" appearing in the film (Camillo, Rospo and Giacomo) are concerned, I'd like to emphasize that Camillo carries out his "Chinese" ideas on a personal rather than a political plane. But he has not become a

"Sinophile" by mere chance: this has been a political choice. Since the film makes an extremely severe judgment on the Italian political situation, we wanted to go right through to the conclusion that in Italy there's no real class alternative as yet, that if there is an attempt to put one together we are still far from any concrete results, that the current crop of small groups on the extreme left (with their magazines, newspapers, etc.) is due more to the clamorous loss of prestige of the Communist Party than to their own force and autonomous necessity, and that therefore such groups are often more in opposition to the C. P. than autonomous of it. (Because this is above all a moment of stasis, of ideological development.) So our "Chinese" is not what he is by chance or paradoxically, because to make him a political leader—meaning a representative of a real alternative political phase—would be objectively utopian.

TATTOLI: Coming back to the subject of the provinces and the metropolis, integration in a national political reality which one opposes is to some extent inevitable. The problem is to reduce it to the minimum necessary for survival, to be as efficient as possible in order to serve the *cause*. Recognizing that this necessary minimum may vary from individual to individual, it can't be denied that there are very frequent abuses, and that the militants who apply this rule rigorously are very few.

CHIARETTI: Let me summarize some of these observations. The young protagonist, Camillo, is not a political leader. He develops his revolt on a strictly family level, or you might say psychological level, or social-psychological. A hypothesis of this sort could be valid not only in the case of a Maoist position, although that is what we have here. (I'd say we have a caricature of it, and you say the same.) But this hypothesis is valid also for any other position that embraces terrorism as a mystique. We have here, that is to say, the infancy of a leader, and the young man who is "Chinese" might also be a Fascist, like so many who at a critical and dramatic moment of their relationship with a conventional and corrupt family feel the need to explode in an attitude of revolt, of scandal, of blasphemy. But being "Chinese" is a precise and not a casual fact, as you say and as you show. You say that the film does not center around Camillo, but around Vittorio if anyone, and you identify in him a process of social-democratization which cuts into different social classes and different parties, and which finds its definition in the generic concept of the Center-Left government coalition. The opposition to this Center-Left cannot come from the Right, or at least you don't want it to. So here we have three boys who are raising the question—even if only with bombs and writings on the wall—of the idea of progress in the direction of socialism, which is supposed to be absent from the Center-Left, *i.e.* from Vittorio, Carlo and the others. Nevertheless, these characters are judged impotent to satisfy revolutionary aspirations, their own or those of the class they intend to defend, represent or stimulate. The conclusion is skeptical. The lack of a real revolutionary alternative might lead us to suspect an attitude of determinism, of wait-and-see, if not a *qualunquistic* type of judgment on the exercise of political *activity* on every level, even when it doesn't tend to *participate* in the exercise of political power.

BELLOCCHIO: I don't believe that saving something is enough to avoid being *qualunquistic*. What counts, for me, is that the tone is neither skeptical nor fatalistic. In *China Is Near* we don't have the person who protests without faith, already foreseeing the futility of his accusations. In the film, the protest is specified every time, detailed, inflexible, *partial*. In the *qualunquistic* attitude there's a parareligious coefficient: justification, comprehension, fore-bearance, and, in the end, complicity on the part of the author, all of which is completely absent in *China Is Near*. It's true that there's not a single standard-bearer of *our ideas* in the film, but this is because, as we said earlier, at this time we can only recognize "what we don't want" (because, I repeat, an *autonomous European strategy* has not yet been developed on the basis of the Chinese experience).

CHIARETTI: But why, after one film that contested on the

one hand the usual mode of considering the family, and on the other, of considering the cinema, have you chosen to make a film that touches on themes of this sort (even if only in a provincial setting)? Perhaps the film is not this, but something else: the crisis of a family, or of a class, or of a social attitude.

BELLOCCHIO: The film describes, basically, an operation of reinforcement of the bourgeoisie, which renews itself by purloining the best youth of the proletariat, corrupting those who would be the natural leaders of the proletariat. Since *Fists in the Pocket* had exorcized a certain adolescent experience, objectivized it, I wanted to turn my research in an opposite direction, to make the discussion more complex and to introduce foreign elements into a bourgeois family pattern. In *Fists in the Pocket* I described the daily life of a family, neglecting its relationship with its neighbors, its servants, etc. In *China Is Near*, the two traditional classes come face to face, and the exploited are the ones who lose out, even if apparently it may seem just the opposite.

CHIARETTI: You're suggesting reading the film almost as an allegory. That is, if I understand correctly, you give a particular value to the character of Carlo as a proletarian corrupted by the action of systematic integration by the bourgeoisie. In reality it seems to me that Carlo doesn't have the psychological make-up of a proletarian, but I understand perfectly what you mean. And it's significant that despite his humiliating actions, you can't dislike him. Both what you've said here and the film itself lead us to believe that you're reproposing the thesis of the *engagé* artist, or at least of the film which contains "didascalic" elements.

BELLOCCHIO: *China Is Near* may be considered "didascalic," but not in the Zdanovian sense (the positive hero, etc.), nor as Rossellini uses the term. (When Rossellini speaks of "didascalic," he means really scholastic, informational, but fortunately he contradicts himself in practice, as in his film on Louis XIV.) This is a "didascalic" film because it tries to show not how to be, and to live, but how not to be, how not to live. Unlike *Fists in the*

Pocket, this should be understood not only through the style, but also precisely through the facts presented, the words spoken, the situations, etc. This film tries to show an example of how the classes only apparently tend toward unification, integration and disappearance, but how on the contrary, for everyone who wins there's always someone who loses, for everyone who gets richer there's always someone who gets poorer, for everyone who frees himself from his own material enslavement there's someone waiting to take his place.

CHIARETTI: How not to live? Not like Vittorio, above all, if I've understood properly. But let's for a moment try to go beyond what the film says. I'll ask you to trace, for "didascalic" purposes, Vittorio's *curriculum vitae*. That is, to fill in some of the suggestions given in his last speech, for example.

BELLOCCHIO: I'll try to make an outline of Vittorio's life, as if the character existed before the film or existed in reality. [1]

1. The choice and vote for the Christian Democratic Party (his first) are the natural conclusion of an uninterrupted brainwashing from infancy through high school, by means of the Catholic Action (Catholic Boy, Aspirant Minor, Aspirant Major, and so on through that hierarchy), the Catholic schools, and the family (economic prosperity and religious observance go hand-in-hand by nature).

Fatalism toward the disinherited ("the poor have always been with us and always will be").

2. But in the first years of (Catholic) university Vittorio confusedly realizes that things are not as he has always been

---

1. In the original screenplay of the film *China Is Near*, Father Comotti outlined for Camillo, in a sort of senile prattle, a curious portrait of the "Socialist candidate" which may be useful, *a posteriori*, for reconstructing Vittorio's itinerary:

"... In '53 I was the spiritual father of you all, and I must say that that silly Vittorio was among the most reverent of all the boys: he served Mass every day and every day he took communion... the Socialist... and like all good boys he had the problem of getting to Heaven. Vittorio certainly wanted to get there, and how!...

"I told him the Sacred Heart of Jesus has promised that whoever took communion for nine Fridays in a row would be assured a holy death; that is, with the comforts of religion.

"As soon as Vittorio heard that, he set to it right away, and even took a tenth communion for safety's sake... where was I, oh... when he informs me, I reassure him, anguished as he is by this problem, that he'll have a beautiful death... because I'm sure he will continue on the right road... I was wrong...

"... But you have to tell him, now that he's blustering so, you have to tell him not to be so sure of a good death, because that comes only, listen to me, my child, if you take communion for the love of God and not to escape the flames of Hell—and having done it one Friday extra argues for the thesis that Vittorino took communion above all to guarantee himself against eternal punishment."

taught, that there exist enormous social inequalities, that he represents a tiny minority, that he is truly a member of a privileged class (unconscious guilt complex). In his abstract, sentimental, self-satisfied search for greater justice, for greater social understanding, Vittorio gives his second vote to the Social Democratic Party (a party in the Center government coalition: property safe). Vittorio would like the rich to acquire a greater social sensitivity "spontaneously." Vittorio "aspires," but does nothing else.

3. But soon he is dissatisfied by this second choice too. His parents die, and his passage to the Communist Party coincides (oddly enough) with his abandoning the administration of the family property to his sister Elena. Vittorio discovers class, the relationship of capital to labor, etc. He reads and gets involved in the life of the Party. Elena is taking care of their interests and Vittorio can permit himself any sort of adventure, any promise, any condemnation of their inherited property. In the eyes of his "peers" he is simply an eccentric. His unconscious aspiration is perhaps to have himself interdicted.

4. The life of the Party begins to bore him; it is always the same thing: discussions in the taverns, the necessity of adapting himself to the conditions of his new comrades (second-class in the trains, cheap seats in the movies; Vittorio can never suppress a certain shame).

The Hungarian episode gives him the excuse to abandon the Communist Party and to pass into the Radical-Republican Party. This is the laical moment: the moralization of public life, the denunciation of corruption, the limitation of the power of the Church, "Catholic de-education," the abolition of the Catholic private schools, the denunciation of tax frauds (some quarrels with Elena). The *Espresso* becomes his ideal weekly magazine.

5. The years pass on, frustrations increase, teaching is boring (to fill his time he teaches philosophy in the local high school). The Chinese cultural revolution explodes and for Vittorio it represents a new burst of idealism.

Vittorio is greatly attracted by China and is about to become a "Sinophile" like his brother Camillo, but just then the local Socialist Party offers him its nomination for the next local elections, with a guarantee of heading a city department. Vittorio accepts instantly and justifies himself to his brother with these words: "Agreed, you are right, but it's futile: the things you believe in, and which in the last analysis I believe in too, will never be accomplished now. To think something's just, but not

to believe it can be accomplished, means one doesn't even believe it's just... so I don't believe in it... I need to do something soon, right away... something in a group, seeing that I've never been able to do anything by myself..." The armchair and the desk in City Hall don't have the same meaning for Vittorio that they would for a party hack. For him they represent the possibility (the illusion) of giving a more dynamic sense to his own life; they mean trying out command, authority, for the first time in his life; they mean reducing for a while the all too common sensation of being useless, of being nothing.

In the meantime the family property is safe in Elena's hands, and is being continually increased so as to be preserved.

CHIARETTI: I understand that while this is extremely useful in order to understand what you had in mind when you began to make the film, this is a dangerous operation as far as a critical analysis goes. One might say that what you've told us is a film still to be made. But you made *China Is Near*. I think it's fairly equivocal to insist too much on the political character of the film. In reality, it seems to me, from certain hints you've given, that there are some points in common between this second film and your first. But there are also divergencies, such as the difference in styles. Without attempting right now to make a judgment that should be more fully worked out, I'd like to observe that while *Fists in the Pocket* fit eloquently enough into an idea of avant-garde cinema (partly due to certain bitter ruptures in the language), *China Is Near* seems on first reading to be based, on the contrary, on a fairly traditional type of narration, that arrives at a contestation of the same thing from within.

BELLOCCHIO: It's a dovetail style. The film is formed rather like a geometric pattern, on parallel lines. There are four real protagonists, two men and two women. The whole film moves on two parallel planes: while one action takes place in one setting, another occurs contemporaneously in another setting. In most cases we wanted to investigate not the settings or the planes, but above all the relationship between one setting and another of the same episode. The bomb, for example: with the Socialist head-quarters and the Catholic school. The reawakening of the house, with Camillo running in the garden, the telephone call to the Socialist headquarters, Vittorio and Giovanna in the library, Elena waking up, etc. The double, contemporaneous seduction (Carlo's of Elena and Giovanna's of Vittorio), the contempora-neous awakening of Carlo and Giovanna, their finding each other on the veranda, their leaving together while their bosses sleep... That is, when we were writing the screenplay Elda and I tried to weave together a number of situations, without worrying about the risk of becoming schematic.

CHIARETTI: There's another difference between the two situations. In *Fists in the Pocket* there's an extreme spatial and temporal freedom. Here, on the contrary, everything is measured with great care and tends toward unity, or to emphasize the existence of continuity in the story. You've given some examples. There are others: Vittorio goes to give a speech in the village and his sister goes to the same village. The young party secretary makes love precisely when the boys go to write on the walls in front of party headquarters.

BELLOCCHIO: Yes, we wanted to force reality, in this sense.

CHIARETTI: Not just to mention names dear to the *nouvelle vague*, but in a certain sense one could think of a Hitchcock-type of style, in which the play of time and place counts for a great deal in the story.

BELLOCCHIO: Of course this "exaggerated contempora-neousness" is a stylistic choice; in fact, were we to compare reality pure and simple, all these coincidences would be quite incredible...

TATTOLI: I'd say it wasn't incredible, given the provincial setting. I'd say, rather, that these things are absolutely provincial: in a small town coincidences are much more frequent than in a large city. Coincidence, that is, is a sort of characteristic of the provinces. Still on the question of the style of the film, I'd like to add that à propos of certain episodes, we might speak of "photographed theater," without wanting to allude to the "primitive" cinema of Méliès or to use this expression in a pejorative sense, as Bresson does. It's a "theatrical" film in the sense that it often wants to demonstrate in words what it contests, in the sense that the dialogue is often conceptual, in the sense that the settings (aside from one or two scenes) illustrate the action like painted backdrops; they never come alive or substitute for the characters (as in Antonioni or Visconti, for example). They are there to serve the characters; or better, to serve their words.

But nevertheless, I think that in some cases, something cinematically autonomous has emerged from this apparently unrefined and primitive technique.

CHIARETTI: But it's always dangerous to say, "Reality is like this." We have here a plot constructed as a screenplay.

BELLOCCHIO: No, it's not that we wanted to say, "Things happen like this in the provinces." It's a concentration of situations.

CHIARETTI: For example, let's take a fairly marginal episode that is relevant to this point: the scene of the seduction of the young party secretary by the lady of the house. You see this episode through an explicitly ingenuous interest in the house, and through the paintings which mirror an imminent sexual encounter...

BELLOCCHIO: But it's not marginal; it's an important scene.

CHIARETTI: I don't mean it's not important. I want to emphasize that it's constructed with *narrative rigor*, as they say, so that it might have come out of (I don't know if this is a compliment or not, in this case) a traditional type of film—a film by Visconti, for instance. I could see an analogous scene in *Vaghe Stelle dell'Orsa*, for example.

TATTOLI: What do you mean? That this scene seems stylistically incongruous?

CHIARETTI: No, it's certainly in the style of the film. What strikes me is the difference between this investigation and that in *Fists in the Pocket*, where the idea would have been represented with totally unconventional means—with a scene just as long, perhaps, but without that almost geometrical precision of the framings and the insets, without so obvious an optical game.

BELLOCCHIO: There we wanted precisely to emphasize a psychological element: he sees her through her possessions. But in a way you're right to cite Visconti. But not the Visconti of *Vaghe Stelle dell'Orsa;* absolutely not.

CHIARETTI: I mention *Vaghe Stelle dell'Orsa* for the reference to a house which has a relationship to the characters through its objects.

BELLOCCHIO: I wanted to show a desire objectifying itself. For instance, we see her appearing on the glass of the portraits of her ancestors. Here is a man who has no background, no nothing, who is zero, and he has this desire to possess a past too; that is, not only a woman, but a woman with all her past.

CHIARETTI: You're right, but I want to tell you that as far as I'm concerned, I prefer sloppy things, when the sloppiness has a meaning, to clean-cut ones. I don't mean to make a comparison between a supposedly sloppy *Fists in the Pocket* and this supposedly clean film; not at all. But I say that the two belong to two different types of cinema. One type tends to be correct, refined, magnificent, like that of Castellani, for one, against whom no objections about *craftsmanship* can be raised. And the other type is what we find in Godard, which I like and which is often wilfully ungrammatical; that is, the image blurs, the camera bounces, and so on—that is, all the things that aren't supposed to be done and that he does. This is the sloppiness of a certain type of avant-garde, that often becomes just a meaningless cliché, an unacceptable affectation.

BELLOCCHIO: For myself, I wouldn't say sloppiness; simplification is more like it. I hope it doesn't seem like simplification in content.

CHIARETTI: Let's get to the point. I wonder whether this attitude, which seems different to me, might not somehow have

been born from your being in different conditions; that is, in conditions of greater security, of greater stability, after a type of success like that of *Fists in the Pocket*. That is, how would you react to an observation of this type: the production side has been assured, and this has influenced the film from a commercial point of view, with the acceptance of certain commercial conventions? How would you react to the doubt that this type of clarity may not be an alibi, more or less conscious, for the fact that the commercial-industrial engagement is greater and therefore the film must go to the public in the best possible conditions?

BELLOCCHIO: The answer is no.

TATTOLI: No, the film has been made with such a production contract (low cost and no profit-sharing) that such suspicions are absolutely groundless. There was never the least consideration of giving the film a greater (commercial) accessibility to insure it greater success with the public.

CHIARETTI: I hope it will be successful. But it's certainly clear that, though "didascalic," the public ought, in order to understand it, to bear in mind a series of things that are not said in it. Unfortunately the situation is as you describe it. So to say "China" *tout court* today is to say something absolutely generic to the public. This distinction you make within the minorities on the left is incomprehensible even to regular readers of newspapers, and even of newspapers which concern themselves with politics. I remember that the *Espresso*, when it interviewed you, couldn't understand what you were talking about, because for the *Espresso*, for the man who writes on cultural problems, this sort of distinction is the jurisdiction of the fellow who writes on political problems. And not even his, because he deals with the big news and not with the minority groups. My question was intentionally provocatory. Because certainly one of the objections raised when Bellocchio announced his film—and raised precisely by a *minoritarian left* in the cultural field—was born of the suspicion: "What's going on here?" It might have been thought that the first film had been a sort of Trojan horse with which to enter the citadel of the cinema. Now we make films with Cristaldi. And since Cristaldi is one of the biggest producers in Italy, it's clear where the road is going to lead. So I ask you explicitly: what is the background here?

BELLOCCHIO: The absolute liberty and independence with which we made this film meant also that we had little money and much responsibility. Elda and I are concretely responsible, in the sense that if the money furnished hadn't been enough, we'd have had to finish and deliver the film at our own expense. (But fortunately this didn't happen.) The formula, which we might repeat with Cristaldi if another occasion presents itself, turned out to be a good one.

Cristaldi, too, very intelligently realized that the only way to leave us completely free (freedom with which we have never wanted to compromise) was the formula of letting a job out to contract, which has few precedents in the "producer-author" relationship, at least in Italy.

Cristaldi's "Vides" company took care of all the complex and innumerable bureaucratic problems involved in making a film; we had, besides the responsibility, the work of organization, which we did personally.

CHIARETTI: If I've understood correctly, it was Cristaldi who first proposed doing a film with you.

TATTOLI: Yes, at first there was a proposal on his part to do a film made and produced entirely by "Vides." We counter-offered to make a film produced by him.

Cristaldi, demonstrating great faith in us, accepted this counter-offer. And he was as good as his word, because, as stipulated in the agreement, he never interfered in our work. During the shooting he simply sent a "Vides" executive to check weekly on the progress of the film, and afterwards, during the editing, he came only when invited.

CHIARETTI: Cristaldi and "Vides" approached you when

you were already talking about a particular film, or generically, about a film to be decided upon?

TATTOLI: Generically. They only made the continuation of the negotiations conditional on the reading of the screenplay. The help of Ennio De Concini greatly facilitated our initial relations with "Vides" and the positive result of the negotiations.

CHIARETTI: If the screenplay had not been approved, would Cristaldi have been its proprietor anyway?

TATTOLI: Yes, unless we preferred to remit the money we'd received up till then.

CHIARETTI: And any modifications of the screenplay?

BELLOCCHIO: This was foreseen too: modifications must be approved by both parties. That is, if there is no agreement on a contestation by the production side, the film could be released all the same, but without my signature.

CHIARETTI: In a case of this sort, which fortunately it seems to me will not occur, would Bellocchio be disposed not to sign the film? That is, in the situation of the Italian cinema today, the idea that a producer is the proprietor of the film and that the director can do nothing but withhold his signature is obviously monstrous. Then I'd like to add: I know that according to your contract you have to deliver the film with the approval of the Censor. What does this mean?

TATTOLI: Yes, we have to deliver it with the approval of the Censor. That is, we alone are responsible for obtaining it.

CHIARETTI: Well, I judge this clause ambiguously. That is, it's obvious that it's a form of pressure. But on the other hand, it's also right that the author himself lock horns with the Censor, and that he consider the problem in the broadest perspective.

BELLOCCHIO: Every time the question of independent cinema comes up, the producers are maligned (for their rapacity, obtuseness, vulgarity, ignorance, incompetence, timidity, etc.).

But to get to the roots of the matter you have to talk about the movie theater. It's the theater operator who decides, who accepts or rejects or boycotts certain types of films. An independent cinema group can be created only if you get hold of a certain number of theaters, otherwise independent cinema is an abstraction. There's no substantial difference between doing a film on your own or with a big producer, or directly with a distributor, or in a thousand other ways, when every one of these variously packaged products is inexorably accepted or rejected by the theater operator on the sole basis of the law of greatest profit. It would really be enough to control only ten theaters in Italy to create an independent production and independent circuit (which has already happened in America, for example). I repeat: the only serious way to talk about this is to begin with the theater operators and not the producers. I'd be ready to join a group campaigning for this idea immediately, to contribute to it, to make films for it. Otherwise, once you've got a guarantee of full freedom (which you can obtain with certain producers), it's substantially the same thing to make a film with Cristaldi or make it risking your own money. Because both Cristaldi, with all his authority, and I with none, have got to obtain the approval of the theater operator, who has neither desire nor interest in bettering or trying to change the public taste, or to anticipate it, but follows it forever until he nauseates it.

CHIARETTI: The operator can blackmail, but he doesn't own the product, unless he's come in earlier. If we consider cinema one of the arts, it certainly is in the most absurd of situations. No painter today paints, even on commission, saying: "When I give you the picture you can do what you want with it." The painter can say, "Put it up anywhere you like, put it in the cellar, or even destroy it, but you can't put another brush-stroke on it or take out one of mine, or cut it in four and show the pieces separately." The producer has the right, the power to do what he wants, and the author has the consolation of withholding his signature. Now the authors of films say they want to modify this situation. But it has to be modified with new instruments. I understand that the problem of distribution is just as serious.

The Screenplay

CEIAD COLUMBIA presents:
CHINA IS NEAR
A VIDES film

Story:	Marco Bellocchio
Screenplay:	Elda Tattoli Marco Bellocchio
Director of Photography:	Tonino delli Colli
Cameraman:	Franco di Giacomo
Assistant cameraman:	Giuseppe Lanci
Musical background:	Ennio Morricone
Musical direction:	Bruno Nicolai
Furnishings:	Mimmo Scavia
Montage:	Roberto Perpignani
Production inspectors:	Rodolfo Frattaioli Ugo Novello
Sound:	Vittorio de Sisti (C.S.C.)
Photographer:	Gianfranco Fontana
Assistant, Montage:	M. Teresa Bernabei
Second Assistant, Montage:	Augusto Aquilini
General organizer for VIDES:	Oscar Brazzi (A.D.C.)
Director:	Marco Bellocchio

Artistic collaboration:	Elda Tattoli
Producer:	Franco Cristaldi

Cast:

Vittorio:	Glauco Mauri
Elena:	Elda Tattoli
Carlo:	Paolo Graziosi
Giovanna:	Daniela Surina
Camillo:	Pierluigi Aprà
Rospo:	Alessandro Haber
Giacomo:	Claudio Trionfi
Furio:	Claudio Cassinelli

All references to facts, persons and places are purely coincidental.

SCENE 1

Headquarters of the Socialist Party: Meeting Room. Inside. Evening.

In the Meeting Room, Carlo, in undershirt and shorts, gets up from a pair of benches which have been pushed together. The room is dark.

Giovanna, in her slip, is looking for her clothes.

GIOVANNA: My family's already eating supper; they'll be worried...

CARLO: Did it ever occur to you, Giovanna, that for once your family can very well stay worried and not get on our backs with their punctuality?

GIOVANNA: ...That's the way they are.

CARLO: Too bad for them...

GIOVANNA: Well, why don't we get married?

CARLO: Two people that love each other are married.

GIOVANNA: And now that you're going to be elected to run one of the city departments...

CARLO: Sure, I'll be rich. You know what a department head gets? All of sixty-eight thousand lire a month.

GIOVANNA: Money's just an excuse.

CARLO: It's a fact of life.

As he dresses, Carlo hands Giovanna a piece of clothing.

CARLO: This is yours...

Giovanna shivers with cold.

They finish dressing in the dark. They are still barefoot and tiptoe on the cold floor.

SCENE 2
Malvezzi House. The old kitchen. Inside. Day.

A large table in the center of the room. On the walls, photographs and portraits of Lenin, "Chinese" posters.

Camillo Gordini, seventeen years old, is examining himself in a mirror hung behind the door.

Off camera the voices of Rospo (Toad) and Giacomo, both eighteen, who are coming in from the courtyard.

ROSPO: Vittorio? Isn't he coming?

GIACOMO: Camillo didn't invite him. Today he doesn't want an audience.

They enter and sit down at the table. At the head of the table sits Camillo, who places before him some typed pages. Giacomo gets ready to listen attentively. Rospo sits tiredly and plays with Jà-Jà, the Gordini's miniature schnauzer.

CAMILLO: ... Certainly the necessity of a daily political presence, accompanied by intellectual precocity—which rightly calls for efforts superior to the average—has distracted us from a problem which will become more and more serious the longer we postpone it: the sexual problem. By sexual problem I mean a coitus non interruptus, in horizontal position, with the body totally extended in length, with the active and self-conscious participation of both parties.

ROSPO: What am I, dreaming?

CAMILLO: We have excluded a priori the possibility of experimenting on a prostitute, in the first place because this would require our acting in the open, in public, so that the bourgeois laws would be able to slander our movement. Secondly, because we would risk being infected with venereal disease, whose consequences would weaken our already exiguous ranks.

Rospo kicks a ball to the dog.

CAMILLO: Rospo, if you don't pay attention I'm going to stop.

ROSPO: You ought to...

CAMILLO: A friend who shall remain unnamed knows a girl by the name of Giuliana with amatory possibilities which, he says, are inexhaustible. According to him, during sexual intercourse she goes into a state of unbelievable ecstasy or hypnotic trance so complete that her partner might be substituted without her noticing it: a perfect experimental laboratory for us.

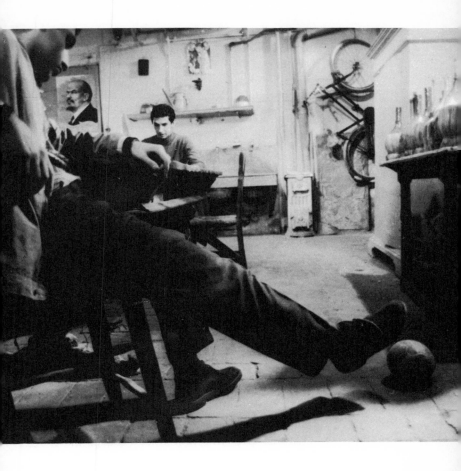

She is from the working class, docile and reserved. Of course a bourgeois girl would be better, so as to ravish in her the class she belongs to. But since the education of such a girl prevents her from going into a hypnotic trance, and since she always has some end in mind when she lets her pants be taken off, we ought to try ourselves out on this Giuliana first.

Furthermore, if Giuliana is a proletarian, she is potentially a petty-bourgeoise.

Let us not forget that, as Chairman Mao says, the peasant class is the only revolutionary class.

Rospo is playing openly with the dog now.

CAMILLO: Oh, cut it out; this is no game.

Camillo gets up and goes out.

ROSPO: He'll be back.

GIACOMO: Well, you could have let him go on; it's such a high-level speech...

ROSPO: Who gives a damn?

GIACOMO: Well, you can't say it's not well written!

ROSPO: Anyway, before you make this kind of proposition you could at least find out if the people you're talking to have the same problems you do.

SCENE 3
Malvezzi House: Bathroom. Inside. Day.

Vittorio, sitting on the toilet, is having some difficulty evacuating.

VITTORIO: My God, my God, why hast Thou forsaken me?

SCENE 4
Malvezzi House: Bathroom. Veranda. Inside. Day.

Vittorio leaves the bathroom with his eyes shut tight; he wants to go back to bed and sleep again.

Annetta comes up to him on the veranda.

ANNETTA: There are two men who want to speak to you, Professor....

VITTORIO: Annetta, don't wake me up... don't ruin me... maybe they want Elena...

ANNETTA: No, no, they want you...

VITTORIO: Of course you don't remember their names... are they from the country?... have they got umbrellas?...

ANNETTA: No, they haven't...

Vittorio reluctantly gives up the idea of sleep and opens his eyes.

VITTORIO: Do you think I can see them in my bathrobe?...

Annetta shrugs her shoulders.

ANNETTA: Well...

VITTORIO: Anyway, ask Elena if she's expecting anyone. In the meantime I'll put on my socks and pants; nobody notices them...

ANNETTA: Should I get your egg ready?

VITTORIO: Why? Are we fasting today?...

SCENE 5
Malvezzi House: Elena's bedroom. Inside. Day.

Elena, awakened by Annetta, has sat up in bed. She is not alone; her companion has hidden under the covers. Annetta has come in and stands in the doorway.

ANNETTA: Please...

ELENA: Who is it? Who is it?

ANNETTA: Your brother wants to know if you're expecting anyone...

ELENA: And you wake me up for that?... And you still listen to all the idiocies that stupid Vittorio says?... Are you crazy?...

You know I have low blood pressure and I'm not supposed to be woken up suddenly like that! Idiot!

Annetta runs out.

ANNETTA: One tells me one thing, the other tells me another.

ELENA: Hey, wake up. Get out of there.

FURIO: I told you it would be better at my house...

ELENA: How many things you've told me, and if I'd done half of them...

Elena gets out of bed and checks through the windowpanes of the door to make sure no one is on the veranda. She goes out onto the veranda (Elena's and Vittorio's bedrooms are adjacent and give onto the veranda, which overlooks the courtyard) and sees Camillo (Vittorio, thirty-five, Elena, thirty, and Camillo Gordini are brothers and sister) down playing with Jà-Jà. Camillo talks to himself as if he were reciting a tragic soliloquy.

CAMILLO: My salvation shall be your salvation... My power... Giuliana, you shall burst my chains, so that my soul shall flow like a river from which you shall drink.

The dog continually disturbs his speech, bringing back the tennis ball that Camillo throws as far away as he can so as not to be interrupted too often. Furio has gotten up from bed and taps on the pane to call Elena back into the bedroom.

Elena comes back inside.

ELENA: What do you want?

FURIO: Can I get washed?...

ELENA: You can't do anything... Go away, it's late; go away before anyone sees you; go on...

SCENE 6
Malvezzi House: Antechamber. Red parlor. Inside. Day.

Vittorio, in his bathrobe, crosses the antechamber to go into the parlor. Borsotti and Alfieri hear him coming and ready themselves to greet him, checking each other's ties.

BORSOTTI: Borsotti, the surveyor...

VITTORIO: ... My pleasure...

ALFIERI: Bernardo Alfieri, the hardware store... Please excuse us, Professor, for coming so early...

Vittorio leads them into the library.

VITTORIO: Not at all, not at all; let's go into the library.

SCENE 7
Garibaldi Street. Outside. Day.

Giovanna, the Gordinis' secretary, rides along on her bicycle. She pedals skillfully and calmly. She wears wool gloves against the cold.

SCENE 8
Malvezzi House: Courtyard. Ground-floor entrance. Outside. Day.

Giovanna bicycles into the courtyard of Malvezzi House, a fine eighteenth century building with brick-and-sandstone façade; it is imposing but not grandiose. The building, taller than all the others in its street, bears the family name of Countess Malvezzi, the deceased mother of Vittorio, Elena and Camillo Gordini.

Jà-Jà runs to greet her, barking. Giovanna dismounts from the bicycle. At the door, she meets Borsotti and Alfieri, who have finished their talk with Vittorio.

GIOVANNA: Hi.

BORSOTTI: Hi.

ALFIERI: Hi.

Giovanna enters the house.

SCENE 9
Malvezzi House: Library. Inside. Outside. Day.

Vittorio is very excited.

Giovanna enters with the cup of freshly beaten egg and hands it to Vittorio.

VITTORIO: Thanks... How are you, Giovanna? Because I'm fine.

GIOVANNA: That's obvious... how come?...

VITTORIO: I'm going to run in the next city elections with the
Socialists...

Giovanna starts.

VITTORIO: ... They've promised me the Department of Education
—guaranteed... Should I accept?

*Giovanna blanches. Camillo has come up to the window looking onto the
courtyard.*

CAMILLO: There's room for you. Give me a spoonful?...

*Vittorio passes him the cup through the bars. Camillo's intrusion embar-
rasses him and dampens his euphoric loquacity.*

VITTORIO: ... When do you go back to school?...

CAMILLO: Tomorrow. You're supposed to take me and you don't
even know?

VITTORIO: Sorry, I'm up in the air. Listen, I'm cold. If you want it,
I'll have another one made up.

*Camillo hands back the cup and goes back to the center of the courtyard,
followed by the dog.*
*Vittorio closes the window and turns to Giovanna with his finger raised
as if to preach benevolently.*

VITTORIO: Let the rich man's repast be frugal, let every table have
its gifts; and let treasure, without proud pomp, go humbly
to the poor man's hut, let it make the poor man's board
resplendent this day appear.

SCENE 10
Malvezzi House: Hallway. Inside. Day.

*Going down a hall which leads to the veranda, Vittorio finds himself
face-to-face with Furio, who is clearly trying to get out of the house.*

FURIO: Oh! Hi, Vittorio. Sorry, we fell asleep...

They hear the dog barking on the stairs and Camillo running up.

VITTORIO: ... Go on, hurry up, before Camillo comes...

FURIO: Sorry...

SCENE 11
Malvezzi House: Elena's bedroom. Inside. Day.

Vittorio enters in a rush and finds Elena having breakfast in bed.

VITTORIO: 'Morning... Couldn't you go to a hotel?... Camillo
    might get a shock...

ELENA: Why should we pay for a hotel if we have a house and no
    one's stopping us?...

VITTORIO: I'll forbid you...

ELENA: You don't count!...

VITTORIO: Listen, Elena: You're as smart as you can be, but you
    don't understand that at seventeen years old one can be a
    Marxist-Leninist but still insist that his sister doesn't screw
    around. What do you expect, we were all that way once...
    The world can be turned upside down but your own
    sister...

*Camillo runs in with Jà-Jà in his arms. He stops at the foot of the bed
and tosses the dog to his sister; Vittorio catches it before it falls on the
breakfast tray and clutches it to his breast.*

CAMILLO: On the fly!

VITTORIO: Look out for the tray!

SCENE 12
Malvezzi House: Library. Inside. Day.

Giovanna at the telephone.

GIOVANNA: Well, anything new?

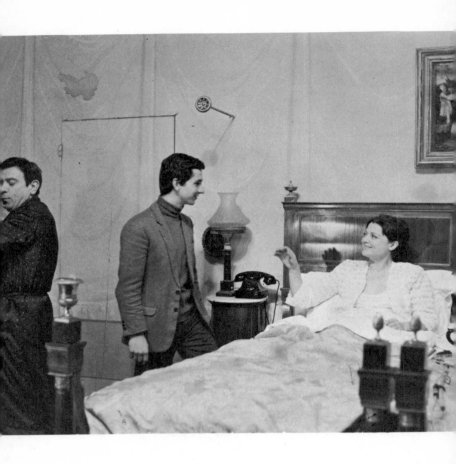

SCENE 13
Socialist Party Headquarters: Carlo's office. Inside. Day.

CARLO: Why? What?

SCENE 14
Malvezzi House: Library. Inside. Day.

GIOVANNA: This morning…

SCENE 15
Malvezzi House: Library. Inside. Day.

Vittorio has come in and Giovanna instinctively hangs up.

VITTORIO: Please go right ahead, don't let me interrupt you...

GIOVANNA: I'd just finished.

VITTORIO: Will you please get me my photograph album?

SCENE 16
Socialist Party Headquarters: Carlo's office. Inside. Day.

CARLO: Hello!...

CLOTILDE: Carlo, Mr. Borsotti's here...

SCENE 17
Socialist Party Headquarters: Main office. Carlo's office. Inside. Day.

Borsotti and Alfieri confer quietly before coming in.

ALFIERI: Are you going to tell him or am I?...

BORSOTTI: Odds or evens?...

ALFIERI: Evens... One two three shoot... it's you.

BORSOTTI: But listen... you come too...

SCENE 18
Malvezzi House: Library. Inside. Day.

Vittorio has just dialed a number and awaits the answer.

Giovanna is stacking photograph albums on the desk, along with loose dusty photographs which she discovers in the drawers of a cupboard.

CARLO'S VOICE: Hello.

VITTORIO: Ah, hello, I'd like to talk with Mr. Carini, the bookkeeper... That's you? Hello... this is Professor Gordini... well, to make it short... you of course know that your party has offered me the nomination... Well, since I'm not very familiar with active politics, I told them I'd like to have a small staff, or at least an assistant, a sort of manager to organize the campaign for me... well, Mr. Borsotti mentioned your name to me...

Giovanna, going through the photograph albums, doesn't miss a word.

SCENE 19
Socialist Party Headquarters: Carlo's office. Inside. Day.

CARLO: ... Would you mind calling me back in half-an-hour; or I could call you... fine, thanks... goodbye...

As he answers, Carlo looks at Borsotti and Alfieri in turn; they have lowered their eyes in embarrassment.

Carlo hangs up.

SCENE 20
Malvezzi House: Library. Inside. Day.

VITTORIO: Thanks, fine, fine, goodbye...

Vittorio hangs up and hurries to help Giovanna, who is having difficulty climbing down the ladder with a large number of albums in her arms.

VITTORIO: Wait, wait, I'll help you.

GIOVANNA: The ones on the bottom...

VITTORIO: Giovanna... Giovanna, are you pleased I'm going to head a department?...

GIOVANNA: I don't care one way or the other.

VITTORIO: What's the matter, Giovanna?... I don't remember saying anything that could've offended you... or did I? Did I? Don't cry...

Vittorio takes her hand and kisses it.

VITTORIO: If I could only forget this damned self-control for a minute...

Giovanna pulls away and hurries off to hide her tears.

SCENE 21
Malvezzi House: Cellar stairs. Inside. Evening.

Rospo and Giacomo speak in low tones.

ROSPO: This is an insane asylum. At Milan they don't give a damn because we're here to nurse him. But just because he gives money doesn't mean he can do just any old thing. How low we've fallen!!

Camillo has been listening in the dark of the stairs.

GIACOMO: Sssh... Shut up...

ROSPO: Well, why did you call me? I told you already I don't want to have anything to do with it.

CAMILLO: First of all, when I give an order you have to obey... is that clear?

Vittorio is coming down the stairs; Camillo blocks his way.

CAMILLO: What do you want?

VITTORIO: What d'you mean, what do I want? I'm getting some wine.

CAMILLO: I'll get it for you, don't worry about it.

VITTORIO: What's going on here? Is it a secret? This is my house.

CAMILLO: Leave me alone, don't bother me, please.

Vittorio pushes him aside and goes to open the door of the wine cellar, from which Wolfgango, a boy with black beard and mustache, appears.

VITTORIO: Who's this?

CAMILLO: Listen, we'll discuss it later... Forget it...

WOLFGANGO: Come on, go in.

CAMILLO: How goes it? Sleeping?

VITTORIO: Listen, Giacomo; after you, of course, can I go in too?...

GIACOMO: Well, I don't know... Ask Camillo.

SCENE 22
Malvezzi House: Cellar. Inside. Night.

Camillo enters the cellar and goes over to the bed where Giuliana waits quietly. Camillo sits down next to her and moves closer as if to whisper in her ear.

CAMILLO: ... Miss... Giuliana... the action which I am about to undertake is not an abuse... now it might even seem like a common and squalid abuse of an innocent minor... but in the last analysis you too will benefit from the advantage I will gain... the just cause which you are helping with your kindness will benefit, in time, even the class to which you yourself belong, helping it to become conscious of its exploitation through me, because I will help it gain class-consciousness... which I will be able to do partly because you in this way are helping me to gain consciousness... Do you understand? Or better, have I made myself clear?... The circle close...

Giuliana, with her eyes closed, embraces him and pulls him down.

SCENE 23
Socialist Party Headquarters: Entrance. Office. Meeting Room. Carlo's office. Bathroom. (All the rooms are adjoining; the office is separated from the Meeting Room by a partition; an opening without a door joins the two rooms.) *Inside. Night.*

Carlo and Giovanna enter in the dark.

CLOTILDE'S VOICE: Someone's here...

CARLO: Wait...

Carlo goes into the office by himself and turns on the light.

CLOTILDE'S VOICE: Carlo, please turn out the light...

Carlo immediately turns out the light and comes back to Giovanna. Taking her by the hand, he pulls her toward the bathroom.

CARLO: I'm sorry, come over here.

GIOVANNA: But where are you taking me?

CARLO: Come on...

GIOVANNA: I don't want to stay here, let's get out of here...

CARLO: I can't, they've already seen me... please stay there.

GIOVANNA: But this is humiliating...

CARLO: Who gives a damn...

Carlo pushes her into the bathroom and turns the key. He goes into the Meeting Room, turns on the light and discovers Clotilde and a boy, who are dressing hurriedly.

CARLO: Who's that?

CLOTILDE: A comrade from the provincial headquarters.

Carlo continues to speak only to Clotilde, as if the boy didn't exist.

CARLO: What is this, a whorehouse?

BOY: Hey, tell your friend he doesn't scare me...

The boy and Clotilde, buttoning her blouse, go toward the door.

CLOTILDE: So long.

CARLO: So long.

As soon as Clotilde and the boy are outside, Carlo goes to the bathroom and opens the door; Giovanna is furious.

CARLO: Don't get mad, I already am myself...

SCENE 24

Via Luigi Sassi. Street of the Socialist Party Headquarters. Outside. Night.

Vittorio is in his car, parked; he looks at his watch.

Camillo, Giacomo and Rospo arrive. Rospo is hiding a can of white paint under his raincoat. Vittorio gets out of the car and gives the keys to Rospo, who gets into the driver's seat. Camillo and Giacomo get in the back seat.

VITTORIO: I'll walk the dog while I wait, but come back right away, will you? It's cold here. Oh, listen, don't go too fast; it's new.

ROSPO: Another slave of materialism.

VITTORIO: I'm still breaking it in...

GIACOMO: We'll break it out...

Vittorio walks off. Giacomo starts the car violently; Vittorio turns back.

VITTORIO: Hey, what do you think you're doing? Forget it, give me the key...

Vittorio gets into the driver's seat.

VITTORIO: It's not your car! Where do you want to go?

CAMILLO: Left... right; look out, you can't get through...

VITTORIO: You trying to teach me how to drive?... What's that smell of paint? Listen, kids, I don't want any trouble: you should have told me first and I'd have given you the car.

CAMILLO: Why, are you afraid?

VITTORIO: What d'you mean afraid? I just want to know where I'm taking you. I'm not your chauffeur...

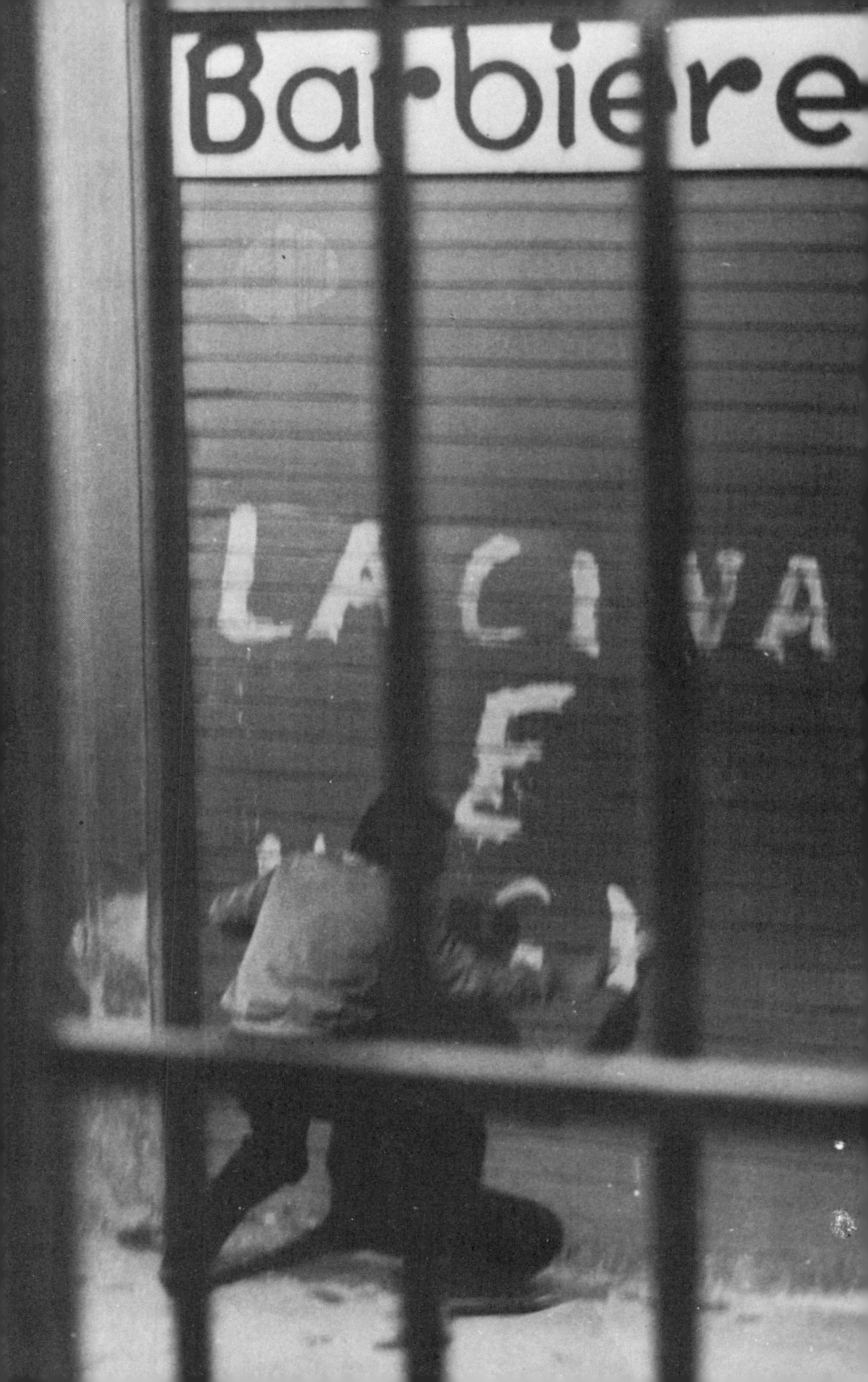
Barbiere
LA CIVA
E

After going through several narrow and deserted streets, the car nears the headquarters of the Socialist Party.

CAMILLO: Here, stop in front of the Socialist Party...

In the instinctive attempt to park as far away from the building as possible, Vittorio suddenly swerves to the opposite side of the street without seeing a car coming head-on; the other driver has to cut suddenly to the wrong side of the street to avoid hitting him. Vittorio stops short and collapses, overcome, on to the steering wheel.

CAMILLO: Hey, are you crazy?

VITTORIO: Did he stop?...

CAMILLO: He's gone on.

The three boys get out. Rospo goes to the right after dipping the brush into the can of paint; Camillo is already on the left. As Rospo and Camillo begin to write on the wall, Giacomo keeps watch to see that no one is coming.

VITTORIO *(inside the car)*: Listen, I'm going...

CAMILLO: Just a second... keep the motor running...

VITTORIO: Sure, what should I wait for?

SCENE 25
Socialist Party Headquarters: Meeting Room. Inside. Night.

Carlo and Giovanna, half-dressed, have been listening motionlessly for a few moments to what has been going on outside. Carlo puts out his and Giovanna's cigarettes on the floor.

Carlo goes to the window, draws aside the curtain and sees Camillo, who has just finished writing on the opposite wall: CHINA IS NEAR

CARLO: Come here, come see your little master, what charming things he's up to...

SCENE 26
Street before Party Headquarters. Outside. Night.

Vittorio sees a night watchman bicycling up from the other end of the street; he puts the car in gear and drives off. The night watchman takes down the number; Vittorio reverses and returns to where he was parked. The night watchman gets off his bicycle and comes up to Camillo and his companions.

ROSPO: Someone's coming. Hey, boys, it's a night watchman; what'll we do?

CAMILLO: Be calm, calm.

NIGHT WATCHMAN: It's prohibited to write on these walls...

CAMILLO: Yes, but look here...

NIGHT WATCHMAN: Write wherever you want to, but not here...

CAMILLO: And why not?...

NIGHT WATCHMAN: Because the Socialist Party pays for surveillance. You can write on that wall or on that other one... that's none of my business; but not on this wall...

CAMILLO: Very interesting...

NIGHT WATCHMAN: And if you don't want me to report it you'll have to erase what you've written right away...

ROSPO: And with what? With our tongues?...

NIGHT WATCHMAN: That's none of my business...

CAMILLO: It's none of his business...

NIGHT WATCHMAN: Let's have your papers, please...

CAMILLO: If you don't cut it out I'll let you have something else...

SCENE 27
Socialist Party Headquarters: Meeting Room. Inside. Night.

GIOVANNA: ... Are you going to stop it?!

CARLO: In my shorts?

SCENE 28
Street before Party Headquarters. Outside. Night.

NIGHT WATCHMAN: Please come with me to police headquarters...

CAMILLO: Please, please... do you like being a slave that much?

NIGHT WATCHMAN: Come on to headquarters and we'll see how funny you are there!...

Vittorio gets out of the car, exasperated.

> ### SCENE 29
> *Socialist Party Headquarters: Meeting Room. Inside. Night.*

CARLO: This is a good one: "Vittorino" our candidate!

> ### SCENE 30
> *Street before Party Headquarters. Outside. Night.*

VITTORIO: Excuse me, y'know, forget it, they're just kids... it's
better to pay the fine...

CAMILLO: Vittorio, we're not paying any damned fine!

NIGHT WATCHMAN: I can't take fines, I don't give out fines...

VITTORIO: All right then, take this... come on.

Vittorio has taken a ten-thousand lire bill from his wallet and put it in the night watchman's hand.

CAMILLO: But if you pay him you're àdmitting we're in the wrong... don't give it to him.

VITTORIO: Shut up or he'll get scared and won't take it...

NIGHT WATCHMAN: No, I don't want it...

VITTORIO: Take it, keep it, keep it... come on, let's not make a scene...

The night watchman hands the bill back to Vittorio.

VITTORIO: Don't make me laugh; come on, keep it, come on.

NIGHT WATCHMAN: No, no; let's go to police headquarters...

VITTORIO: Look, my good man, you've already taken it, I'm sorry, take it back, it's as if you'd already accepted, there are no saints.

NIGHT WATCHMAN: Look, I gave it back...

VITTORIO: It doesn't count that you gave it back; for the law it only counts that you took it... and look, I have three witnesses here who will certainly testify in my favor, so the least that can happen is that you'll lose your job: decide for yourself...

NIGHT WATCHMAN: I didn't take it, I didn't take it...

VITTORIO: You took it, you'll be tried for it... come on, take it...

Vittorio puts the bill back in his hand.

NIGHT WATCHMAN: No, I don't want it...

VITTORIO: But you already took it, you took it a second time...

All right, here, here's another; keep it; they're yours, can't you understand?!

NIGHT WATCHMAN: But I don't want it...

This time Vittorio puts the bills in his pocket.

VITTORIO: You don't want it and you've got it in your pocket; how can you not want it if you've already taken it in your hand twice and once in your pocket... did you take it or didn't you? You took it!...

CAMILLO: Vittorio, control yourself!...

The night watchman, with the money in his pocket, jumps on his bicycle and races away. Vittorio, sweating, looks around and by chance glances at the window from which Carlo is watching; Carlo moves back into the shadow but Vittorio sees the curtain move.

VITTORIO: Someone's inside!

GIACOMO: Let's get out of here...

Before getting into the car Vittorio kicks the can of paint.

VITTORIO: Get rid of it... it's the corpus delicti...

ROSPO: Oh hell, we haven't murdered anybody!

They get into the car, which drives off rapidly.

CAMILLO: Rospo, don't sit on the dog.

SCENE 31
Socialist Party Headquarters: Meeting Room. Inside. Night.

Carlo and Giovanna have dressed.

CARLO: Vittorio is a college graduate and I'm a bookkeeper... the party list had to get more high-toned, they needed a "professor," a college grad. So I lost the nomination and the

department to a capitalist who will reassure the petty-bourgeois voters...

GIOVANNA: One more reason for us to get out...

CARLO: Jesus Christ, Giovanna, let's not get on that again... get out, get out; you get out!... if you haven't already understood, I like to live in this stinking town, and I want to stay here, where for so many years I've been living with less than what's necessary; one day I want to have much more than what's necessary: the more I have to put up with the more I want.

GIOVANNA: You don't have to tell me...

CARLO: Yes, I think I have to... up to now we've just been playing, as if love were something outside our daily lives, outside our jobs, our bosses, our miserable class: a false joy, a false enthusiasm. I want to get into the saddle, Giovanna! I'm through with holding the stirrups.

GIOVANNA: So are you going to work for Vittorio Gordini?

CARLO: For now.

GIOVANNA: You talk and talk... and then when you should be saying no...

CARLO: Don't worry about me, Giovanna; I know what I want.

SCENE 32
Street: Newspaper stand. Outside. Morning.

Vittorio buys a newspaper and looks through it, then closes it quickly.

SCENE 33
Classical High School: Second-year mixed class. Inside. Morning.

Vittorio, sitting at his desk, opens the newspaper. A girl leaves her seat and comes up to him. Vittorio shuts the paper rapidly.

GIRL *(softly)*: Excuse me, Professor, could I look at the syntax book?

VITTORIO: Go right ahead...

Vittorio reopens the paper and looks at his picture. A boy leaves his seat and comes up to his desk. Vittorio closes the newspaper.

BOY: Excuse me, Professor, could I look at the syntax book?

VITTORIO: No.

BOY: But you told the Romanelli girl she could...

VITTORIO: So I told her. So what?

BOY: But...

VITTORIO: Go on, sit down... You know I don't like to have the janitor sit in my place, because I want to believe in your sense of responsibility.

Vittorio gets up and goes to the door.

SCENE 34
Classical High School: Bathroom. Inside. Morning.

Vittorio, in the toilet, opens the newspaper. Moved and pleased, he savors the article written about him. The headline is, "A Millionnaire Candidate for the Socialists."

Vittorio folds the newspaper and puts it back in his pocket. One foot on the toilet, his hand on his chin, he is blissfully meditating on his future when his eye falls on a mangled copy of the Gazette *which has clearly been put there to substitute for the missing toilet paper. He looks more closely; it is that same day's issue. Vittorio flips through the pages with his foot until he comes to the page with his article, crumpled and sodden.*

SCENE 35
St. Barnabas' School: Chapel. Inside. Evening.

The students crowd behind the rail; they smile and joke in low tones as they wait to kiss a fragment of St. Barnabas' clothing, preserved under glass in a precious reliquary which the priest offers for their lips, murmuring an invocation at each contact. Camillo escorts him, dressed as an altar boy; he is clearly fibbing as he answers with the same parsimony of voice.

PRIEST: Sancte Barnaba.

CAMILLO: Ora pro nobis.

Giacomo and Rospo enter.

ROSPO: Let's give him a surprise!

They kneel down with the others.

ROSPO: Fee fie fo fum, I smell the blood of a Christiun...

The priest goes on with his office. Rospo suddenly doesn't feel like playing any more.

ROSPO: What're we doing? Let's get out of here.

Rospo doesn't get up in time. The priest makes him kiss the relic.

ROSPO: It always ends up this way.

The ceremony ends. After removing their vestments, Camillo and the priest return to the chapel. Giacomo and Rospo, who have sat down on a bench to wait for Camillo, rise and go up to him.

CAMILLO: ... How did you get here?...

GIACOMO: ... With your brother...

CAMILLO: Where is he?...

GIACOMO: In the sacristy paying your board...

The priest walks toward the confessional.

PRIEST: Gordini, I'm waiting for you.

PRIEST: Gordini, are you ready?...

CAMILLO: Coming, Father.

GIACOMO: I'll go...

CAMILLO: ... If we don't teach Vittorio a lesson this week we'll forget everything, we'll make it up...

Giacomo kneels at the confessional; a grate separates him from the priest.

PRIEST: What do you have, dear boy, to denounce?...

GIACOMO: I denounce you first of all, if you're so frank as to ask me what I should denounce...

PRIEST: No... what sins do you denounce, I mean...

GIACOMO: I denounce myself for not denouncing you and I pardon myself for this denunciation... but I still denounce you for not letting me denounce you...

PRIEST: I have the impression you're not well disposed toward the sacrament... or am I wrong?

GIACOMO: I'd be well disposed to be well disposed if I could dispose of a good disposition, but being ill disposed to be well disposed, obviously I have no disposal to be well disposed...

Vittorio enters the chapel with a priest; he goes up to Camillo and they embrace.

VITTORIO: Hi, how are you?

CAMILLO: Drop dead...

VITTORIO: Hey, take it easy.

CAMILLO: Father, I just remembered I have to take Ricciardi's place with Father Comotti...

VITTORIO: I'll go with him.

CAMILLO: Who asked you to come?

A priest turns to Rospo.

PRIEST: Do you want to confess?

ROSPO: No, no.

PRIEST: Take your hands out of your pockets.

SCENE 36
St. Barnabas': Father Comotti's apartment (antechamber, bedroom, music room). Inside. Evening.

Camillo carries a tray with Father Comotti's supper. Vittorio is with him. Vittorio continues along a corridor leading directly to the music room without going into the priest's room.

VITTORIO: Listen, I'll wait for you in the music room. I don't want to listen to the usual paternal lecture.

CAMILLO: Go on, go wherever you want!

Camillo crosses the antechamber and meets Ricciardi coming out of Father Comotti's room.

RICCIARDI: Is this the time to come?... They'll have taken my place at ping-pong.

Ricciardi goes off.

CAMILLO: Go on, play ping-pong and learn something.

Camillo enters the bedroom; Father Comotti is deaf and Camillo must shout to make himself understood.

FATHER COMOTTI: Gordini, what is it?

CAMILLO: Broth and chicken.

FATHER COMOTTI: What?...

CAMILLO: Broth and chicken... I'll fix it for you...

Father Comotti, propped up in bed on several pillows, holds a copy of the Gazette with Vittorio's picture.

FATHER COMOTTI: ... But is it true what the paper says, that your brother's gone in with the Socialists?...

CAMILLO: Very Socialiiiist...

Camillo sets the tray on a table in the music room, where Vittorio has been waiting.

Camillo begins to cut up a quarter of a boiled chicken.

Vittorio keeps carefully out of the priest's line of sight.

VITTORIO: Do you need any money?

CAMILLO: Money, money, you always think you can fix everything with money...

VITTORIO: Well, do you or don't you?

CAMILLO: Of course I do, and I want it because it's mine too.

VITTORIO: Who's saying it isn't?... Camillo, will you cut out this act?!...

CAMILLO: You even dare raise your voice?...

VITTORIO: I can understand you're disappointed at my political choice...

CAMILLO: You'd already made a political choice, and you've betrayed it for a mess of pottage...

VITTORIO: No, Camillo, there's always been a big misunderstanding here. I joined your group in a very special way, out of affection, or family feeling, or I'd even say paternally...

CAMILLO: We don't need any Daddy Vittorio.

VITTORIO: That's not what I said...

CAMILLO: And you'll find that out!...

VITTORIO: Because in reality I have always been a moderate progressive—laical, yes—a radical more than anything...

CAMILLO: And you're not ashamed of it?!...

VITTORIO: And therefore appearing in the Socialist list is perfectly in line with my ideas.

CAMILLO: Father, do you want anything more?

FATHER COMOTTI: No, I'm not up to it.

CAMILLO: Father, here are the Virgin's Little Chicks...

A group of younger pupils have come in to visit the priest.

FATHER COMOTTI: Good evening, boys. Hello, hello. And now, let's sing "A Ray of Love Appeared" like good boys. Come on, like good little boys.

The children gather round the bed. Camillo is at the piano; Vittorio sits next to him. The children begin to sing. Father Comotti listens in rapture; now and then he marks the beat with his hand.

VITTORIO: ... The things you believe in, and which in the last analysis I believe in too, will never be accomplished now... to think something's just but not to believe it can be accomplished means one doesn't even believe it's just... so I don't believe in it... I need to do something, soon, right away... something in a group, seeing that I've never

been able to do anything by myself... I agree, I don't
believe in what I'm doing, I have to laugh at myself a
little, but I keep on doing it, so I do believe it... it's all old
stuff, and here I am wanting to have a little bit of
authority without infringing on the principles of liberty
and democracy...

The music ends.

FATHER COMOTTI: Gordini!...

Camillo leaves the piano and runs to the priest's bed.

FATHER COMOTTI: Gordini, did you see? I counted them. There're
fewer of them than yesterday...

Father Comotti takes a box of candy from the night-table and hands it to Camillo to distribute to the children.

Camillo stands at the bedroom door. The boys come up to kiss Father Comotti, some on the hand, others on the forehead or on the cheek; then they pass by Camillo to take their candy.

LITTLE CHICK: You don't happen to have a butt?...

CAMILLO: A kick in your pants...

VITTORIO: I'm going, so long...

SCENE 37
Country road: Vittorio's car. Outside. Inside. Day.

Carlo, at the wheel, and Vittorio. A fast convertible honks and passes them.

VITTORIO: ... That was my sister... She looks after the property... we have three farms out this way.

CARLO: ... She's very pretty...

VITTORIO: Yes, but she'll never get married; she's too afraid they're after her money...

The convertible pulls ahead and is lost to sight.

VITTORIO: Naturally I hope the cops will be there; I wouldn't want anyone to start throwing rocks...

CARLO: It's not necessary, it's never happened yet...

VITTORIO: In any case there must be a police headquarters in the village; do they know we're coming?...

SCENE 38
Village square: Vittorio's car. Outside. Inside. Day.

The car has parked in a semi-deserted square. Carlo gets out to take a look

around; the square is in the center of a small town at the foot of a medieval fortress.

CARLO: Here we are... Aren't you coming?

VITTORIO: There's no one here... where's the platform?... and the cops?

CARLO: ... Look, Professor, maybe you've attached too much importance...

At this moment a boy, about ten, calls Carlo.

GASPARINO: I'm Gasparino, sir, Robiola's son...

CARLO: Robiola's the local secretary... What do you want?

GASPARINO: My father says that because it was raining yesterday, today he has to finish the sowing and then he'll come and meanwhile I'm supposed to help you...

CARLO: But we can't wait for him; we have three other speeches to make this morning...

VITTORIO: A dirty trick...

CARLO: You have to be patient with them, Professor; they're ignorant...

VITTORIO: But there's all kinds of ignorance; here a promise has been broken; here there's complete, pure and simple disdain for the things they've undertaken to do... no police, no representatives of the party, no platform, no audience...

CARLO: If I have to tell you the truth...

VITTORIO: Now the truth begins to come out...

CARLO: Here the custom is that the speaker takes the mike and begins to speak; you give speeches so as not to make a poorer show than the other parties, but it's not that that brings in votes these days...

VITTORIO: Agreed, but if there's no audience there won't be even this minimum usefulness...

CARLO: Just start and you'll see, someone'll come...

VITTORIO: Not on your life; I'll start only when there are at least... say fifty people; that'll do it...

CARLO: You want them to gather round nothing?...

VITTORIO: Don't try to teach me about life, Carini: I'm no kamikaze for the Socialist Party and I don't intend to make myself ridiculous...

CARLO: What d'you mean ridiculous... at worst they'll ignore you...

VITTORIO: Then will you please tell me what I'm doing here?... talking to the birds?

Carlo, followed by Gasparino, enters a bar and returns with a table, which he places in the quietest part of the square. Gasparino follows, carrying a bottle of mineral water and a glass. Carlo returns to the car and takes out a microphone, loudspeaker and a poster with Vittorio's portrait displayed between the Socialist Party symbols. He sets up the apparatus with great experience and nonchalance, drapes the poster over the table and tests the microphone.

Vittorio, who has not moved from the car, follows all these operations and cannot but admire the absolute freedom with which Carlo moves.

BOY: Will you sing us a song?

CARLO: Keep away, go to school, go home, go on...

A soap vendor accosts Vittorio in the car.

VENDOR: Soap?...

VITTORIO: No thanks...

VENDOR: Three for a hundred lire...

VITTORIO: No, I'm not interested...

VENDOR: My friend, with all respect, take them, it's a bargain...

VITTORIO: Look, will you leave me alone?!

CARLO: In just a few moments, Comrade Professor Vittorio Gordini of the United Socialist Party will be speaking here in this square...

Carlo returns to the car.

CARLO: ... Well?...

VITTORIO: Is that all there are?... a mere handful...

In fact, despite the announcement, not more than fifteen people have gathered round; among them is a group of very vivacious children.

CARLO: Come on, Professor: let's go...

VITTORIO: Let's go, my ass!...

CARLO: Then admit you're scared shitless...

Vittorio, furious, gets out of the car.

VITTORIO: Come back here! I won't allow you to insult me and give me orders... *(to the vendor who is standing by watching)* and what do you want? Go away...

CARLO: I said it to give you courage…

VITTORIO: I've got courage to spare…

CARLO: Well, show it…

Vittorio walks toward the table, but hasn't the courage to turn toward the public.

PEASANT: Turn around, Professor, we're over here!

VILLAGER: He's looking at the scenery.

The people laugh. Vittorio turns around. A boy grabs the microphone.

BOY: Testing! Testing!

CARLO: Get out of here, damn it! Just what we need. Shall we begin? In just a few moments Comrade Professor Vittorio Gordini of the United Socialist Party will be speaking in this square.

VOICE: Hurray!

SCENE 39
Village square: Bar. Outside. Inside. Day.

Elena enters another bar on the same square, in slacks, muddy boots and jacket. The speech being given by her brother barely fifty yards away does not interest her.

FACTOR: Good morning, Countess.

SCENE 40
Village square. Outside. Day.

CARLO: Professor Vittorio Gordini, candidate for the next elections for City Council, will speak for the United Socialist Party. Professor…

Elena has appeared at the doorway of the bar.

ELENA: Idiot!

CARLO *(to Vittorio)* : Better make it short.

SCENE 41
Village square. Outside. Day.

Vittorio has clutched the microphone which Carlo has put in his hand, and is looking straight ahead. There are only a handful of people in the audience. The children, who are in the majority, do not appear to have serious intentions of following the speech; they continually move about, shove each other, talk loudly and laugh. Vittorio takes some papers from his pocket; they are folded in four, and as he tremblingly unfolds them, one slips out of his hand and flutters to the feet of a boy who picks it up and flees on his bicycle.
Vittorio chases him. With a burst of speed he catches the boy and hits him. The square instantly comes alive. Idlers, shopkeepers and passers-by arrive to defend the boy, the innocent, the fellow-citizen.

VILLAGER: Since when do they hit kids?... I'll take care of him.

VITTORIO: That kid had even worse coming to him...

CARLO: What're you saying, Professor, these people aren't kidding...

VILLAGER: Socialist my foot! I'll break your face for you...

Carlo intervenes at the first shoves.

But they are surrounded; the first pushes increase in number and violence.

SCENE 42
Village square: Bar. Inside. Day.

Elena is talking with the factors.

FIRST FACTOR: At least thirty oxen.

SECOND FACTOR: At least.

The street-cleaner enters.

STREET-CLEANER: Countess, they're beating up your brother.

The factors race outside, followed by Elena.

FIRST FACTOR: Hey, they're not kidding. Hey, are you guys crazy?

Carlo and the factors take hold of Vittorio; breaking out of the circle, they get him out without too much damage and head for the nearest bar, with Elena following. Someone locks the door; the crowd gathers outside the door.

VITTORIO: What hoods!

CARLO: Where's the phone?

BARMAN: Back here.

VITTORIO: Damn you! Damn you!

CARLO *(on the telephone)*: Hello, sergeant, this is Carini... Listen, could you send someone over? No, nothing, a bit of trouble. The usual Stalinists who've provoked us. Mostly it's that the Count doesn't have much experience. But nothing serious.

ELENA: Take it easy, Vittorio; you want a drink?

VILLAGERS *(from outside)*: We're waiting for you; we'll give you what's coming to you... come on, come on out...

VITTORIO: Of course I will; I'm not afraid of you...

ELENA: Vittorio, forget it, you've already gotten into enough trouble...

VILLAGER: Come on, we'll fix you! Let's go get his car!

CARLO *(on the telephone)*: Just annoying. Goodbye.

VITTORIO: No, no, I don't let this sort of thing go by.

CARLO: Take it easy, Professor, take it easy.

VITTORIO: What d'you mean take it easy?!

CARLO *(to Elena)*: You're the Professor's sister.

ELENA: Yes, pleased to meet you.

CARLO: Will you have something?

ELENA: Of course, if it hadn't been for you...

CARLO: Your brother is a little inexperienced. And so nervous too.

SCENE 43
Village square. Outside. Day.

The villagers wreck Vittorio's car: windows and lights are broken and the body dented by kicks.

SCENE 44
Bar. Inside. Outside. Day.

Vittorio watches, horrified, as his car is wrecked. He goes out on the terrace of the bar.

VITTORIO: Carini! Carini!... How much have I got to suffer for this damned election: if it'd ever even just crossed my mind, I'd never have... They're wrecking my car, Carini...

CARLO: No, no, it's just to make you go out... it's a trick.

VITTORIO: Carini, I can't stand it, I can't stand to see it wrecked like that for nothing... Once a car has been to the garage it's not new any more; it's not new any more...

SCENE 45
Village square. Outside. Day.

Vittorio cannot stand to see his property ruined under his very eyes; he goes out of the bar in a rage.

CARLO: He's out of his mind...

VITTORIO: I'm no coward! I've got to fight!

Vittorio is again surrounded: the men begin to push him again.

VITTORIO: Bastards! Hoodlums! I'll have you all arrested!...

The pushes cease and the punches begin to fly; Vittorio defends himself covering his face.

Carlo comes outside and gets into the fight.

VITTORIO: I told you we'd need the cops!

SCENE 46
Malvezzi House: Living Room. Library. Red parlor. Inside. Evening.

Elena, in her bathrobe, cuddles up on the couch watching television. She drinks a cup of tea which she has just poured.

Giovanna is typing in the library.

ELENA: What are you doing at this hour, Giovanna?

GIOVANNA: ... It's publicity for your brother...

ELENA: Please bill all this overtime to the party and not to me... Do you want a cup of tea?

Through the windows on the courtyard Giovanna sees Vittorio's car driving up; the headlights flash in all directions as he parks. Vittorio taps on the windows to ask Giovanna to open the door.

VITTORIO: Giovanna, Giovanna, would you open the door? I've forgotten my keys.

ELENA: Who is it?

GIOVANNA: It's the Professor.

Giovanna runs to open the glass door of the red parlor. Vittorio enters, followed by Carlo; both are black and blue and scratched. Despite his obvious exhaustion, Vittorio walks with his head held high, like a gladiator leaving the arena.

VITTORIO: Are you still up?... Giovanna, this is Mr. Carini...

GIOVANNA: Hi...

CARLO: Hi...

Giovanna betrays her surprise; Carlo, on the contrary, remains aloof, as if waiting to see what type of behavior will be most opportune.

VITTORIO: You already know each other?... that's a funny coincidence...

GIOVANNA: Yes. Do you want to give me your coat?

CARLO: Thanks.

VITTORIO: Make yourself at home, Carini.

SCENE 47
Malvezzi House: Living Room. Inside. Evening.

Vittorio, Carlo and Giovanna have come into the living room. Elena remains seated.

VITTORIO: Hi. You already know Mr. Carini, don't you?

ELENA: Hello.

CARLO: Hello.

ELENA: Please sit down. Do you want some tea?

VITTORIO: Not me.

ELENA: And you, Mr. Carini?

CARLO: Yes, very much, thanks.

ELENA: Giovanna, will you please serve.

Giovanna serves the tea.

ELENA: How did it end?

VITTORIO: The cops took everything down, as usual, but nothing will come of it... the only annoying thing is the car: it'll take fifty thousand to fix it, at the very least... anyway... there's nothing to do about it. Listen, Giovanna, when you've finished, of course, would you mind drawing me a bath?

GIOVANNA: Yes, of course...

VITTORIO: I know it's not part of your job... and you could refuse to do it...

ELENA: Why do you keep on reminding her, if you make her do it every time anyway?...

VITTORIO: What's that got to do with it? If you'll excuse me, I'll put on a robe... Carini, can we offer you a bath too?

CARLO: Ah, I'd really like that, but I wouldn't want to put you to too much trouble.

Giovanna follows Vittorio out of the living room.

VITTORIO: There's no hurry...

Carlo looks about him as he sips his tea. Holding the teacup and saucer, he rises to admire closer up every single object in the room.

CARLO: With your permission I'd like to look around...

ELENA: You can leave the saucer...

CARLO: ... This house is really beautiful...

ELENA: You like it?

Carlo is observing a moth-eaten velvet shoe preserved in a glass case like a relic.

By chance Elena's face is reflected in the glass; she feels free, behind his back, to observe him with particular interest.

Carlo notices it and is pleased.

ELENA: Are you spellbound?

CARLO: What is it, a shoe?

ELENA: Yes, it's the shoe of a pope who gave it to the family...

CARLO: Imagine how much time and how much money it took to put all these things together...

Giovanna is about to re-enter the living room.

ELENA: Giovanna... bring the tray back to the kitchen... And do
    help yourself too.

Giovanna picks up the tray and goes out with eyes lowered.

Carlo stands before the bust of a pope.

CARLO: Is this the same pope that gave you the shoe?

ELENA: No, another pope.

Carlo continues to look around; he sees Elena's reflection in a series of small family portraits lined up on a well above a large couch.

CARLO: All your ancestors?

ELENA: Yes.

He looks at Elena, who has come up to him; he embraces her and they fall onto the couch together.

SCENE 48

Malvezzi House: Library. Inside. Evening.

Giovanna has begun to type again. The water continues to run in the bath-tub. Vittorio appears at the door in a bathrobe.

VITTORIO: Giovanna, you work too hard... have you marked down all the overtime?

GIOVANNA: Don't worry about it... you'd better go, the tub must be full by now...

Vittorio comes up to Giovanna, who continues to type.

VITTORIO: All right, I'm going... Giovanna, if you could have seen how we fought this morning... life should always be like that: violent, dangerous... that's the word... Giovanna, the naked eye doesn't see it, but it's all a matter of fists and punches here... stop typing a minute... Giovanna, give me your hand; I kiss it, I kiss your hand; don't pull away... not that you don't have the right to... Giovanna, may I lean my head on your shoulder?

GIOVANNA: Professor, if you don't hurry the tub will run over...

VITTORIO: ... Giovanna, couldn't you come and scratch my back?... I know it's not one of your duties...

GIOVANNA: Go on, Professor, go on...

VITTORIO: ... I'm going.

SCENE 49

Malvezzi House: Red parlor. Living Room. Inside. Evening.

As he crosses the red parlor on his way to the bathroom, Vittorio notices through the door that the lights have been turned down in the living room. Curious, he enters and sees, unseen, Elena and Carlo together on the couch. He immediately goes back to Giovanna.

SCENE 50

Malvezzi House: Library. Red Parlor. Inside. Evening.

VITTORIO: Giovanna!... stop typing!...

Giovanna pays no attention. Vittorio paces rapidly up and down the room, trying to control his excitement.

VITTORIO: Stop it, stop it!...

He takes her hands from the keyboard and clutches her arms, forcing her to stand up.

VITTORIO: You know what my sister and Carini are doing in there? They're kissing, they're kissing with all their might... Why couldn't we do it too?... Giovanna, what do you want? Everything?... I'll give you everything...

He continues to hold her with one hand as he takes up the objects he now enumerates with the other.

VITTORIO: Giovanna, do you want this book?... Ten books? Do you want this library? What do you want? This barometer? Not a loan, a gift: do you want this antique inkstand? What do you want? Come on, tell me what you want. You want money? I'll give it to you. Giovanna, I could fire you... Giovanna, I'm on my knees... I kiss your shoes... Giovanna...

GIOVANNA: Get away, clown.

VITTORIO: Clown to me? How do you dare?

Vittorio flees with his hands in his hair.

Giovanna bursts into tears. On tiptoe, she crosses the red parlor and looks through the crack between the door and the jamb into the living room, where she sees Elena and Carlo; she watches for a few moments.

Vittorio's voice is heard singing: "Dormirò sol..." (Don Carlos).

SCENE 51
Malvezzi House: Living room. Inside. Evening.

Carlo and Elena embracing on the couch.

CARLO: Listen, Giovanna will have fixed my bath by now.

ELENA: Go on, I'll wait for you in my bedroom.

CARLO: I won't take long.

SCENE 52
Malvezzi House: Stairway. Corridor. Bathroom. Inside. Evening.

Giovanna races up the dark stairway, crosses the corridor and reaches the bathroom door. She knocks with decision. Vittorio, already in the bath, gives a start and stops singing.

GIOVANNA: Professor, open up, open up...

VITTORIO: What's happened?

GIOVANNA: Open uuuup...

VITTORIO: I'm coming, I'm coming, give me a minute...

Vittorio, trembling, gets out of the tub, envelops himself in a bathtowel and opens the door a crack.

Giovanna pushes the door open; seeing her so upset, Vittorio is frightened. Giovanna does not speak.

VITTORIO: What's happened? If it's an accident, tell me right away, don't keep me in suspense...

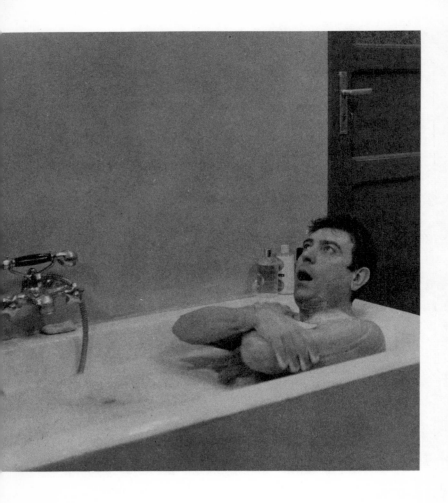

As he talks, Vittorio dries himself, but he does not want to uncover himself in Giovanna's presence.

Vittorio is so clumsy in his attempt to reconcile two materially contradictory actions that Giovanna bursts out laughing, and begins to unbutton her blouse.

VITTORIO: Did you change your mind? What's so funny?

His pride wounded, he wants to embrace her to demonstrate all his virile self-confidence: he opens his arms, and the towel, abandoned, slips to the floor, leaving him naked.

Giovanna laughs, as he embraces her.

SCENE 53
Malvezzi House. Stairway. Corridor. Bathroom. Inside. Evening.

CARLO: Giovanna, Giovanna!

Carlo tries to figure out where the noise of running water is coming from; he goes up the stairs and enters the corridor. Giovanna, earnestly kissing Vittorio in the bathroom, hears him coming.

VITTORIO: It's Carini; what'll we do?

GIOVANNA: Are you afraid of compromising yourself?...

VITTORIO: Of course not!

Carlo, who may have heard the voices, raises his own:

CARLO: Giovanna, where are you?... Where is this bathroom?

VITTORIO: It's me, Carini... Giovanna, button up, hide...

GIOVANNA: Where?... down the drain?...

VITTORIO: Giovanna, don't ruin me, don't humiliate me in front of a subordinate... What do you want, Carini?

CARLO: I can't find the bathroom... could you tell me...

VITTORIO: It's in the back of the house...

GIOVANNA: ... I'll show him...

VITTORIO: But you're mad... Giovanna, have you lost your head?...

CARLO: Maybe I should ask Giovanna... but I don't know where she is either...

GIOVANNA: Here I am!

VITTORIO: Giovanna, don't go, I beg of you...

But Giovanna has already freed herself and opens the door. Carlo is before her; Vittorio manages to hide. Giovanna goes out and closes the door behind her.

GIOVANNA: I'll show you the way...

Her appearance leaves no doubt: her blouse is outside her skirt and a strand of hair has fallen into her eyes. Carlo, for his part, displays the same sort of disarray.

SCENE 54
Malvezzi House: Servants' bathroom. Inside. Evening.

Giovanna leads Carlo into the bathroom (a narrow servants' bathroom). Giovanna turns off the water, tests the temperature, checks that there are soap and towel, and lays the bathmat next to the tub.

Carlo takes her by the arm as if to speak to her; Giovanna repulses him violently.

GIOVANNA: Don't try that any more... and don't look at me like an idiot... haven't you ever seen me before?!

CARLO: Look, Giovanna, you're the one that's making a mistake, not me... can't you understand you can't just do as you please, you haven't got a thing of your own and you have to live by your work; if you get known as someone who gives it away you won't find a dog to marry you...

GIOVANNA: Why, aren't you going to marry me?...

SCENE 55
Malvezzi House: Elena's bedroom. Inside. Dawn.

Elena and Carlo in bed. Elena wakes up and looks at the clock.

ELENA: Hey, wake up.

CARLO: What time is it?

ELENA: Five. You have to go, I wouldn't want anybody to see you.

CARLO: Will I see you tomorrow?

ELENA: You're coming here anyway, aren't you?

CARLO: Yes.

ELENA: All right, then we'll see each other. Now go and don't make any noise.

SCENE 56
Malvezzi House: Vittorio's bedroom. Inside. Dawn.

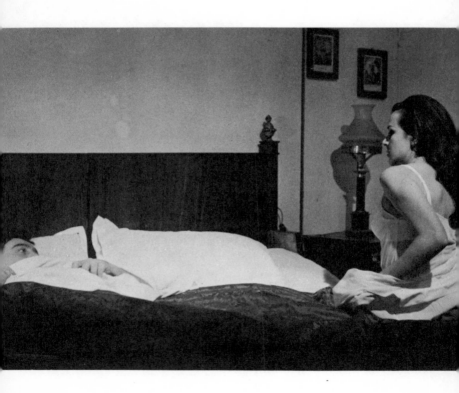

Giovanna gets out of bed, gathers up her clothes from the floor and dresses; Vittorio raises himself up on the pillow.

VITTORIO: Can you get home alone all right?

GIOVANNA: Yes, yes, of course...

VITTORIO: Remember, absolute silence. Sorry, you know, but I think it was a mutual agreement. You're free and I'm free. But this doesn't mean...

GIOVANNA: I understand.

VITTORIO: Giovanna, please. Close the door.

GIOVANNA: So long.

SCENE 57
Malvezzi House: Veranda. Inside. Dawn.

Giovanna comes out on the veranda and finds Carlo sitting on a chest tying his shoes. Without a word she sits next to him and arranges her appearance.

SCENE 58
Malvezzi House: Veranda. Inside. Dawn.

Carlo and Giovanna are about to leave.

Jà-Jà comes up to them from the end of the veranda; barely awake, she stretches and yawns. She wants to go out with them; they shut her in.

SCENE 59
Socialist Party Headquarters: Antechamber. Office. Meeting Room. Entrance. Bathroom. Inside. Evening.

Clotilde has finished her day's work. She covers the typewriter, yawns, stretches and removes her smock. The offices are in shadows. Clotilde goes to the bathroom to tidy up before leaving. As she crosses Carlo's office she does not notice Giacomo watching her from outside the window that opens on the inner courtyard. Giacomo goes around to the front door, where Rospo is waiting.

GIACOMO: All clear...

Rospo enters the headquarters with a briefcase under his arm (the front door is always open during office hours). He crosses the antechamber and the office and hides in the Meeting Room. Clotilde comes out of the bathroom. She closes the front door behind her. As she leaves, she passes Giacomo pacing up and down in the entrance. She does not notice him. Rospo comes out of his hiding place. He recrosses the office, the antechamber and Carlo's office, and enters the bathroom. He climbs up on the toilet. He opens the briefcase and takes out a package. He unwraps the package, which contains a time bomb. He winds up the time mechanism, sets it and places the bomb in the tank, just above the water line.

SCENE 60
Socialist Party Headquarters: Meeting Room. Office. Antechamber. Carlo's office. Inside. Day.

A crowd is gathered in the Meeting Room: delegates from the entire province are meeting in view of the elections. Several persons are seated around the President's table, facing the rows of seats; Vittorio and Carlo are among them, sitting side by side.

PRESIDENT:... which has been born of the need to break the twenty-year-old immobility which the two traditional blocs—the Christian Democrats and the Communists, from the Government side and from the Opposition— have imposed on Italian society.

Rospo enters the adjoining room dressed as a messenger boy; he hands a telegram to Clotilde.

ROSPO: Telegram. Sign here.

PRESIDENT: This autumn has seen the unification of all Italian Socialists, and our Constituent Assembly has opened to

all the masses the proposal of a great party of the Left which—as the statutory rules have recently sanctioned—will guarantee respect for ideas and freedom of opinion to all minorities within the party.

SCENE 61
Socialist Party Headquarters: Entrance. Outside. Day.

Rospo goes out into the entrance, and after closing the front door, secures the two portals with a heavy chain and a lock.

SCENE 62
Socialist Party Headquarters: Meeting Room. Office. Antechamber. Inside. Day.

Clotilde waits for the President of the assembly to finish his sentence before handing him the telegram.

CLOTILDE: There's a telegram.

PRESIDENT: Thanks.

The President opens it and reads it aloud.

PRESIDENT: "Dear conventioneers, in three minutes a time bomb will blow up the headquarters and you with it..."

DELEGATE: It must be a joke!

Most of the delegates are worried; a small minority are incredulous. But all rise and rush to the door.

SCENE 63
Socialist Party Headquarters: Entrance. Outside. Day.

Rospo immediately drives a refrigerator van up against the door so that its metallic side cuts off all possible escape. Giacomo helps him, signaling the manœuvers and risking being caught between the door and the side of the truck. Rospo jumps down from the truck and locks the doors.

Note: Although there are no specific examples in the screenplay, in the film itself the behavior, dialogue, faces, dress, etc. ought to make clear the difference among the minds and the practical efforts of the three revolutionaries. Giacomo is the most timid and ill-adapted to the role he plays (he is entirely dominated by Camillo and belongs to the same social class). Rospo, the only one who has stopped studying and has gone to work, is the most practical and also the most courageous—the only one in whom "revolutionary anarchism" represents not only a violent reaction to family frustrations or a misguided education, but also, even if confusedly, a real political "objectivity."

SCENE 64
Socialist Party Headquarters: Meeting Room. Office. Antechamber. Carlo's office. Inside. Day.

While some of the delegates try to break down the door with kicks, shoves and every sort of manageable furniture, the others, led by Carlo, have run into his office to telephone. But before anyone can raise the receiver, the telephone begins to ring.

DELEGATE: What're you waiting for? Answer!

CARLO: It's an old trick. If we answer they block the line.

DELEGATE: But it's already blocked if it's ringing.

CARLO: Wait, it'll stop.

SCENE 65
St. Barnabas': Father Comotti's room. Inside. Day.

Camillo is at the telephone in Father Comotti's bedroom; the priest is resting and another schoolboy is keeping him company.

OPERATOR'S VOICE: They don't answer... shall I keep on ringing?

CAMILLO: ... There must be someone there...

OPERATOR'S VOICE: You're sure you have the right number?...

SCENE 66
Socialist Party Headquarters: Carlo's office. Inside. Day.

Carlo's tactics do not convince the delegates.

THIRD DELEGATE: It must be my wife...

CARLO: Let's wait.

THIRD DELEGATE: I'm sure of it... Hello! Hello!

The delegate cannot resist and grabs the receiver, on which Carlo's hand has been resting. No one answers from the other end of the line; the telephone is useless and the confusion increases. Most of the delegates move about in herds; many crowd against the windows and call for help (the headquarters is on the ground floor and all the windows are barred).

Some have already panicked; no one jokes any longer. Vittorio, apparently in control of himself, is alone in a corner of Carlo's office.

SCENE 67/A
St. Barnabas': Father Comotti's room. Inside. Day.

Camillo, at the telephone, snickers silently. His companion would like to get in on the fun, but Camillo does not let him near.

FATHER COMOTTI: Gordini, don't they answer in the sacristy?

SCENE 67/B
Socialist Party Headquarters: Inside. Outside. Day.

The delegates talk to the people outside through the windows.

DELEGATE: Hey! Call the police.

CROWD: We already have.

Some of the delegates have succeeded in opening the door, but the side of the truck adheres perfectly to the opening, barring all exit.

DELEGATE: Let's crawl under...

ANOTHER DELEGATE: Don't you see, there's the step?

A Capuchin friar stops and from the sidewalk tries to comfort the less serene among the delegates.

The news of the bomb spreads.

The people outside leave the window and withdraw to the opposite sidewalk.

The Capuchin remains.

Traffic continues to pass by.

A fight for the telephone breaks out in Carlo's office; each man believes he knows the right word to make the person on the other end of the line desist.

In the midst of the uproar, the only one to keep his head is Carlo, who runs back and forth searching in the drawers, in the cupboards and in every possible hiding place: he is looking for the bomb.

Someone thinks of making the Capuchin friar talk on the telephone; they call him to Carlo's window so they can pass him the receiver.

FIRST DELEGATE: Father, do something.

CAPUCHIN: But what do you want me to do?

SECOND DELEGATE: Let's get him to talk on the telephone.

THIRD DELEGATE: Why? What do you want him to say?

SECOND DELEGATE: A priest is always an authority. A Capuchin is better yet.

CAPUCHIN: What is it? What's going on?

SECOND DELEGATE: A bomb.

CAPUCHIN: Why are you shouting? What have you done? Is anyone hurt?

SECOND DELEGATE: Father, come over to the courtyard window.

CAPUCHIN *(on the telephone)*: Hello!

SECOND DELEGATE: It's someone who doesn't want to talk. Tell him not to be an idiot!

CAPUCHIN: My son, to tell... to tell the truth, the situation is not yet perfectly clear to me...

DELEGATE: Get to the point, Father, get to the point.

SECOND DELEGATE: The time is almost up...

CAPUCHIN: ... My son, in the name of God, to tell you the truth I haven't yet understood what's going on, but I beg you to talk if you have the gift of speech, because here there's a great confusion of souls, a great lack of grace...

OPERATOR'S VOICE: ... Are you talking?...

CAMILLO'S VOICE: Yes, yes.

CAPUCHIN: A voice! God has illuminated him...

A delegate grabs the receiver from the Capuchin's hand.

DELEGATE: Where's the bomb? We heard you! Talk or I'll murder you!

SCENE 68
St. Barnabas': Father Comotti's room. Inside. Day.

The Rector enters while Camillo is on the telephone.

RECTOR: You know it's forbidden to call from the school? You know it or don't you?

CAMILLO: Yes, Father.

SCENE 69
Socialist Party Headquarters: Inside. Outside. Day.

DELEGATE: Devil take you and that whore of your mother!

CAPUCHIN: What are you saying?!... It's not his mother's fault...

SECOND DELEGATE: The time's run out...

THIRD DELEGATE: Not yet...

CAPUCHIN: The mother is a lily... a lily...

SCENE 70
St. Barnabas': Father Comotti's room. Inside. Day.

RECTOR: And naturally it'll be a long-distance call... and if I hadn't caught you you'd never have told the office...

SCENE 71
Socialist Party Headquarters: Carlo's office. Inside. Day.

CARLO: Come on, stand back, give him room, let him talk.

CAPUCHIN: Oremus...

Vittorio, trembling violently, detaches himself from the wall, makes his way to the telephone, takes the receiver and lifts it to his ear.

SCENE 72
St. Barnabas': Father Comotti's room. Inside. Day.

RECTOR: Who are you calling?... Eh?...

CAMILLO: ... Home...

The Rector grabs the receiver from Camillo and listens.

SCENE 73
Socialist Party Headquarters: Carlo's office. Inside. Day.

Vittorio, urged on by all the delegates, does not know how to begin. Carlo understands that he needs a minimum of privacy and moves back a few yards with the other men.

SCENE 74
St. Barnabas': Father Comotti's room. Inside. Day.

The Rector listens; Camillo trembles; the doctor is talking with Father Comotti. The Rector begins to lose patience with the long silence.

SCENE 75
Socialist Party Headquarters: Carlo's office. Inside. Day.

Vittorio ends his hesitation.

VITTORIO: ... This is Vittorio...

SCENE 76

St. Barnabas': Father Comotti's room. Inside. Day.

RECTOR: It's your brother...

The Rector hands the receiver back to Camillo and goes over to the doctor.

RECTOR: He was calling his brother Vittorio...

FATHER COMOTTI: I know him well. The Socialist.

SCENE 77

Socialist Party Headquarters: Carlo's office. Inside. Day.

VITTORIO: ... Is that you or isn't it?... at least tell me, I'm your own brother... in all conscience, is this any kind of joke to play?... haven't you already had your fun?... is this you or isn't it? When will it go off? I'm in Carini's office, am I safe here? Have I got time to talk?... The point is that this isn't where you should be putting bombs... your real enemies, the ones you should really be harassing, are the Communists... can I go on?...

CAMILLO: Of course!

The Capuchin prays.

SCENE 78

Socialist Party Headquarters: Carlo's office. Inside. Day.

VITTORIO: ... That is, the official Opposition; that is, the Opposition that doesn't feel like opposing any more... is there still time?... if this bomb is here it's the same as if you'd put it under the Tomb of the Unknown Soldier... the wrong place... what will it cost you to tell me where you put this damned bomb?... we're already dead; do you need to kill us again?... blow up a Communist cell and then you'll be the ones to represent the only dangerous opposition...

BORSOTTI: This is just the time for a family chat.

The Capuchin prays.

SCENE 79

St. Barnabas': Father Comotti's room. Inside. Day.

Camillo can't hold out any longer: the Rector is still only a few yards away from him, even if for the moment he is not paying any attention to Camillo. Above all, Vittorio's words have upset him; once more, without his yet being aware of it, Camillo is being brusquely undeceived.

CAMILLO: ... It's in the toilet...

He hangs up.

SCENE 80

Socialist Party Headquarters: Carlo's office. Bathroom entrance. Inside. Day.

Vittorio too hangs up, after a moment's hesitation. The bathroom opens directly onto Carlo's office, where most of the delegates have gathered. Vittorio and Carlo are at the telephone; all stare at Vittorio.

VITTORIO: Let's go in there...

In the same instant the bomb explodes, blasting out the bathroom door; clouds of smoke billow into the rooms, enveloping and confusing the delegates. They gasp for breath as they try to find something to lean against; they call each other and cry for help.

SCENE 81

Malvezzi House: Dining room. Inside. Evening.

Vittorio is speaking quietly with Carlo at the entrance to the dining room;

he alludes to his two aunts, nuns, who are already seated at the table waiting for dinner to be served. Annetta walks back and forth with the final preparations.

VITTORIO: ... Marina and Lauretta Malvezzi...

CARLO: All right.

VITTORIO: How many are there?

CARLO: Two hundred and fifty-four.

VITTORIO: Well, not bad, is it? Do keep on.

CARLO: All right.

Carlo disappears into the antechamber and Vittorio takes his seat at the dinner table.

VITTORIO: Dear little aunts, how are you? So here I am; I'm at your service.

LAURETTA: Dear boy, our fine boy. To make it short, we stopped in at the Curia today and we talked with the Bishop again, for the sake of scruple...

VITTORIO: A farce...

MARINA: Vittorio, you'll have to resign yourself; we can't vote for you...

LAURETTA: It's not possible.

VITTORIO: A pure and simple farce... anyway, dear little aunts, you can't say yes one day and no the next, because I'm compiling the list of preference voters[1] and if you tell me yes, I'm going to count on your votes too, don't you understand?! and if you don't vote for me afterwards, I get it in the neck, do you understand?! I can't keep hanging on your daily scruples: no one is indispensable, so tell me now once and for all: yes or no and let's be done with it...

LAURETTA: ... But we've already told you...

MARINA *(at the same time)*: ... You don't know it, little boy, ... they haven't told you yet...

VITTORIO: What's Giacosa got to do with it?...

MARINA: That long is the way... and but an hour is Life... and before, alas, you reach the peak... your hands shall be torn, your face bloody with strife...

VITTORIO: Lay it on! Keep going, eh?

---

1. In the Italian system of proportional representation, the voters may express preferences among the candidates of the party whose list they chose; the seats won by each party are assigned according to the number of preferences accumulated by each candidate on the party's list.

MARINA: That you shall bear abuse and sorrow, that today is called dawn and sunset tomorrow...

Annetta enters with the soup tureen.

VITTORIO: Sunset, yes, sunset.

ANNETTA: Countess, shall I serve you?

MARINA: Thank you.

VITTORIO: Annetta, pour me a glass of wine!...

As Annetta pours his wine, Vittorio notices that she is crying.

VITTORIO: What's wrong with you now?... are you crying?...

MARINA: It's that she too would like to be freed...

VITTORIO: What what what?... as God is my judge if you don't vote for me I'll fire you!... have you been working on her too? Freedom, freedom... look, I'll kick you out... I warn you...

MARINA: Don't you have any compassion at all?...

VITTORIO: The compassion of Pharaoh!

Annetta's quiet sobbing erupts at this point.

VITTORIO: ... No, no... I was joking... don't get scared... I've never fired anyone... Oh God how exhausting...

Elena comes to the table; she is in a robe; her make-up and hair show particular care.

ELENA: Good evening, everybody. Vittorio, hurry up and finish eating, you still have to dress...

VITTORIO: No, I'm going like this...

ELENA: You'll put on tails or you'll sit in the balcony... did you persuade them?...

VITTORIO: Of course not... I'd have to terrify them, blackmail them... but what can you expect?...

Vittorio stops eating, letting his spoon fall clumsily into his soup.

VITTORIO: ... Because it pains me, it pains me a very great deal to lose your votes, of two aunts who bear the same name as my mother... will you try to understand that I'm going to be in the seat you elect me to, I with your same blood, I who have thirty-five years behind me, which cannot but reassure you, I and not the party, not the idea, because there are no more parties, there are no more ideas; because things will go on exactly as they are. You just have to read "Populorum Progressio" to realize that even the Pope is much further left than we. Because you still haven't understood...

ELENA: Stop it, Vittorio, you're getting on my nerves...

AUNTS: Well! Poor boy.

VITTORIO: This is certainly casting pearls before swine...

LAURETTA: Thanks, that's very kind of you.

ELENA: ... Annetta, are we going to have the entrée or not?...
Why don't you get Giovanna to help you?

VITTORIO: ... Giovanna isn't supposed to serve; she's not a maid,
she's a secretary...

ELENA: But if she's always done it!

VITTORIO: But it's an abuse!

ELENA: Talk, talk, innocent...

MARINA: We could give a hand...

VITTORIO: You have to give your vote, that's all... Anyway I'm
going to change: I've lost my appetite... to see certain
things... Giovanna is a secretary and not a maid, she's a
secretary, not a maid.

*As he leaves the dining room, Vittorio passes Giovanna coming in with a
tray. Silence returns as Giovanna serves.*

ELENA *(to an aunt):* Would you like some?

MARINA: Yes, thanks.

GIOVANNA: I'll put it here.

  SCENE 82
*Municipal Theater: Orchestra. Stage. Boxes. The Gordinis' private box.
Inside. Night.*

The musicians tune up; the house lights are already out.

People are still coming in.

Vittorio is alone in a box.

The audience applauds the conductor, who bows from the pit.

Elena enters the box; Vittorio takes her hand and sits her down in front of him.

The prelude to "Macbeth" begins.

ELENA: ... I'm already bored to tears with this...

VITTORIO: ... Why don't we rent out the box?... the city is full of do-nothings who'd like nothing better and at least we'd get something out of it...

ELENA: You'd be the first to back out.

Someone shushes them from another box.

Elena rises and sits again behind Vittorio, at the darkest point in the back of the box. She whispers in his ear.

ELENA: Vittorino... I'm pregnant.

VITTORIO: Carlo?...

ELENA: ... And just at this time... with all I've got to do, I had to have this happen to me... and all by myself... why don't you help me find a way?

VITTORIO: ... I wouldn't know where to turn; I've never had any experience...

ELENA: You'd just have to make a few phone calls... and you find the right person right away... it's a man's job, isn't it?

VITTORIO: Carlo will take care of it, if it was him... oh this is just lovely...

ELENA: But he doesn't want to, the fox... and I was so stupid as to go and tell him... he changes the subject... he talks about the danger, puts it off... but he's crazy if he thinks he can trap me...

VITTORIO: ... What a devil of a bookkeeper, if he reckons even on other people's bellies... Count on me, but don't make me take any initiatives...

ELENA: That's a nice line... as usual I'll have to manage all by myself...

VITTORIO: Not in town...

ELENA: I'll take what I can find, my boy...

SCENE 83

Malvezzi House: Dining room. Inside. Night.

The cloth is still on the table, with the oil and vinegar, the salt, the wine and the water, the napkins and the breadcrumbs.

Carlo and Giovanna are eating left-over cake in silence.

Giovanna finishes first and clears the table.

GIOVANNA: ... Do you want any more?

CARLO: No; look here... I have to talk with you...

GIOVANNA: All right.

SCENE 84

Malvezzi House: Living room. Inside. Night.

Giovanna goes into the living room and waits for Carlo to take the initiative. She collects the pages of the newspaper scattered on the couch, folds the paper back together and glances through it.

They sit next to each other on the couch.

CARLO: ... What's happened is... look, I'm talking to you frankly because I think it's all over now between us and we can be friends... what's happened is that Elena is pregnant... she wants an abortion and I'm against it... Let me explain: you keep a lookout on Elena all day long, watch her phone calls, check her mail, make her appointments... that is, I'm asking you to keep watch on her... to know what she plans to do.

GIOVANNA: ... But you don't really give a damn for Elena, do you...

Carlo hesitates.

GIOVANNA: Tell me the truth, it can't change anything.

CARLO: ... Think what you like, but Elena—I like Elena... Of course if she didn't have the money she has maybe I wouldn't care one way or the other... of course I like her with all her money, but I like her... I like her the way she is, that's what... that is, it's not that I like her money and not her... I like both of them together, which isn't quite the right way to put it either. So will you give me a hand? Naturally you won't go unrewarded for a service of this kind...

GIOVANNA: That's just what I was going to say... you know I'm sleeping with Vittorio... except that he is terrifically scared that what's happened to Elena, for example, might happen to me... and naturally he does everything possible to avoid it... so to speak frankly, if you want Elena to marry you because she's pregnant, I want Vittorio to marry me too. So you have to make me have a child.

CARLO: ... It feels like we're playing a game... But it'll all go to hell if we both do it...

GIOVANNA: Then why you and not me?

CARLO: Because it was my idea.

GIOVANNA: So much the worse for you if you told me...

CARLO: ... Jesus Christ, Giovanna... and suppose it's not the right time for you today; do we have to start again tomorrow?

GIOVANNA: Why, aren't I supposed to be keeping watch on Elena tomorrow?

SCENE 85
Municipal Theater. Inside. Night.

Last act of "Macbeth".

SCENE 86
Malvezzi House: Living room. Inside. Night.

Carlo is sitting on the couch; Giovanna is still lying down. Carlo is half-dressed; Giovanna is still in her underclothes.

The noise of a car driving into the courtyard. Jà-Jà, who has been sleeping in an armchair, wakes and pricks up her ears.

Carlo notices the dog's attention.

CARLO: Come on, get up. Get dressed, it must be them...

Giovanna kisses him, and embraces him with great ardor.

GIOVANNA: ... If I didn't get dressed... your whole plan, eh?...

CARLO: Our plan...

GIOVANNA: What d'you think I care... But you'd even break my head for me for that kind of a joke...

CARLO: In any case it wouldn't bring me back to you...

GIOVANNA: Who wants you?...

Giovanna puts on only her sweater, skirt and shoes; she gathers up all her underwear and hides it under a cushion.

SCENE 87
Malvezzi House: Entrance. Inside. Night.

Elena and Vittorio come in from the ground-floor entrance.

ELENA: The light's still on...

VITTORIO: Giovanna and Carini are still working...

ELENA: Since you've gone into politics the light bills and the phone bills have doubled... Close the shutters.

Vittorio stays behind to shut them and sees Elena trying to open the living room door.

ELENA: It's locked!

SCENE 88

Malvezzi House: Living room. Inside. Night.

Carlo turns on the television and goes to open the door. Elena enters.

CARLO: Hi!

ELENA: How come the door was locked?

CARLO: It couldn't have been!

ELENA: Yes it was locked.

CARLO: No it wasn't.

ELENA: Well!

CARLO: How come you're home so early?

ELENA: Bored. *(To Giovanna)* Give me the paper.

Vittorio enters.

VITTORIO: Well, what was the matter with the door?

CARLO: The lock must have gotten stuck.

ELENA: Well, I'm going, good night. *(To Carlo)* Are you coming up?

Carlo follows her.

CARLO: Good night.

VITTORIO: Good night. *(To Giovanna)* Shall we go to bed too?

SCENE 89
Malvezzi House: Library. Red parlor. Inside. Afternoon.

The telephone rings in the library. Giovanna is crossing the red parlor to serve the coffee in the living room; she places the tray on a table at hand and goes to the telephone. Elena arrives from the living room almost immediately and takes the receiver from her hand before Giovanna has a chance to find out who's calling. Elena's action is almost clumsy, and betrays apprehensiveness and lack of self-control.

ELENA: Give it to me. Hello. Go on out.

Before taking the tray Giovanna pours out a cup of coffee: Elena, at the telephone, does not speak, as if Giovanna's presence inhibits her.

GIOVANNA: I'll leave you a cup...

ELENA: Go away, I told you... *(Into the phone)* Yes, yes, what time is it now?

SCENE 90
Malvezzi House: Living room. Inside. Afternoon.

Elena's order to Giovanna has been heard in the living room as well, where Carlo and Vittorio are immersed in reading the newspapers.

Giovanna enters with the tray.

VITTORIO: Sit down, Giovanna, please make yourself comfortable. And serve yourself too, of course.

Giovanna sits on the couch and serves the coffee first to Vittorio and then to Carlo, and finally to herself. She picks up a page of newspaper which has fallen to the floor. Elena calls Vittorio from the library, and he hurries to her.

CARLO: ... Elena is out of her mind...

GIOVANNA: I noticed. I'm afraid we're close...

CARLO: ... Have you looked at her appointment book?...

GIOVANNA: Yes, but there's nothing particular in it...

Vittorio re-enters, not at all calm.

VITTORIO: Carini, I'll change my jacket and we'll go now... the guns are already in the car... In the meantime, take the car out of the garage, if you don't mind...

Vittorio tosses the keys to Carlo and goes out. Carlo and Giovanna rise.

CARLO: Listen. I'll call you from the shooting range... or else you call me there if she sends you out... Understand?

GIOVANNA: ... They've given me the day off...

CARLO: Anyway, stay in the house as long as you can.

GIOVANNA: All right.

CARLO: So long.

SCENE 91
Malvezzi House: Living room. Inside. Afternoon.

Elena, alone in the living room, closes the newspaper; Jà-Jà tries to entice

*her into playing with the ball. Elena gives in a few times without enjoyment,
then takes the dog in her arms and leaves the living room.*

SCENE 92
Shooting range: Field. Bar. Outside. Inside. Afternoon.

*Carlo and Vittorio arrive; a shooting match is under way. A loudspeaker
calls the contestants up on the shooting platform; they are shooting at
sparrows. Five containers stand on the ground twenty-five yards away from
the marksman, who does not know which of the five will open and must
watch all of them. The game seems simple enough because no one misses. A
boy recovers the dead sparrow each time and substitutes a live one taken from
a large cage; the dead bird is abandoned on the edge of the field.*

The obvious self-satisfaction each of the men displays immediately after shooting, their triumphal return to the group standing by watching, their way of blowing down the barrels and snapping the shotguns shut are particularly sinister.

Carlo, carrying the guns and followed by Vittorio, walks into a small building that forms part of the shooting-range complex and contains a bar on its ground floor.

CARLO: Come on in, Professor.

SCENE 93
Malvezzi House: Elena's bedroom. Inside. Afternoon.

Elena has gone to bed. The dog sleeps next to her. Elena checks the time continually; she is agitated and worn out. She seems to hesitate before the telephone on the night table, then she picks up the receiver and dials a number.

SCENE 94
Malvezzi House: Library. Inside. Afternoon.

Giovanna has remained in the library; she has gathered together her things and is ready to leave, but she is still at her desk, staring at the telephone; she has heard a soft ring: someone is using the other phone. Cautiously she lifts off the receiver and listens to Elena's conversation.

SCENE 95
Malvezzi House: Elena's bedroom. Inside. Afternoon.

ELENA: Hello, is Dr. Valla there?...

NURSE'S VOICE: The doctor has a patient right now...

SCENE 96
Malvezzi House: Library. Inside. Afternoon.

Giovanna is at the telephone.

ELENA'S VOICE: Tell him that Miss Gordini says...

The doctor's voice comes in immediately.

DOCTOR'S VOICE: But Miss, I told you not to telephone during office hours.

ELENA: I know, I know, but I don't feel well. Could I come a little earlier?

DOCTOR'S VOICE: I can't before six; come on, keep your chin up and take a tranquilizer; goodbye...

Elena hangs up vexaciously and is immediately invaded by the sadness and discomfort provoked by the idea of the imminent abortion.

SCENE 97
Shooting range: President's office. Outside. Bar. Inside-Outside. Afternoon.

PRESIDENT: ... It's been operating for thirty years now and no one ever bothered us until, as you no doubt know, there was that accident when that maniac began shooting the hunters instead of the birds...

VITTORIO: I remember, I remember it very well...

PRESIDENT: ... Then the Communist newspapers blew the thing up, and the S.P.C.A. got into it, photographs of dead birds, accusations of atrocities, etc. etc.... so the members are worried and want someone who will offer them guarantees...

VITTORIO: I understand...

The telephone rings on the President's desk.

PRESIDENT *(to Carlo)* : It's for you...

Carlo takes the telephone as the President continues to talk.

Vittorio's entire attention is diverted to Carlo's telephone call; Carlo prudently speaks only in monosyllables, neutralizing Vittorio's presence.

GIOVANNA'S VOICE: She's about to go to Dr. Valla. The address is in the phone book, but if you want it...

CARLO: Tell me... tell me.

GIOVANNA'S VOICE: Prof. Francesco Valla, Physician, via Verdi 14... she's going at six...

CARLO: O.K. Thanks for everything, goodbye.

GIOVANNA'S VOICE: I'm going now.

CARLO: Will you be at home?

GIOVANNA'S VOICE: Yes, goodbye.

Carlo hangs up.

PRESIDENT: And then, Count, you don't have to write it in the party platform...

CARLO: Excuse me, I'll be right back... Goodbye.

VITTORIO: Where are you going?...

Carlo goes out without explanations.

He thinks for a moment outside the bar.

He runs to the car.

He drives off.

SCENE 98

Shooting range: Field. Outside. Afternoon.

Vittorio comes out to the range with the President.

It is Vittorio's turn; the boy runs to replace the sparrow killed by the preceding marksman; he runs off the field.

The field is free.

Vittorio takes aim.

One of the five containers opens.

At the second shot the sparrow falls.

SCENE 99
St. Barnabas': Visiting room. Inside. Afternoon.

Camillo and Carlo are talking together at the far end of the immense visiting room; they speak in low tones and cannot be overheard. Camillo's expression is stupefied. An elderly lady walks up and down the room with a small boy, her nephew.

CARLO: Hello.

CAMILLO: Hello.

CARLO: Excuse me if I've disturbed you, but it's something fairly serious. It's about your sister Elena.

NEPHEW: What did you bring me?

AUNT: I've brought you candy, but listen, you ought to be treated very well here. I've given a tip to the doorman and another to the nurse. I've given the Rector a beautiful book and I've made an offering for the chapel. So you ought to be treated as well as can be.

CAMILLO: And who's the father?

CARLO: I don't know, but at this point it doesn't matter.

CAMILLO: And in my heart I couldn't think why she shouldn't still be a virgin.

NEPHEW: Hi, Gordini... Aunty, that boy's a Chinese.

AUNT: A Chinese. What do you mean? He's a European, an Aryan. What do they teach you in school?

NEPHEW: He's a Chinese Communist.

AUNT: A Communist! In such a respectable school! It's incredible. If you're telling me the truth I'll talk to the Rector and take you right home. How are you doing in school? You know if you don't study you'll never amount to anything.

CARLO: If you act like that we won't settle anything, you know.

CAMILLO: Yes, you're right.

CARLO: Let's go.

CAMILLO: I have to get permission.

CARLO: Ah, if you wait for permission...

CAMILLO: You lead the way.

SCENE 100

Malvezzi House: Elena's bedroom. Inside. Afternoon.

Camillo has come into his sister's bedroom as she is about to go to Dr. Valla's.

ELENA: What are you doing here? Eh?

CAMILLO: What am I doing? Why shouldn't I stop my sister from ruining herself? Because you'll ruin yourself, you'll ruin yourself!...

ELENA: I'm not ruining myself, I'm saving myself; listen, Camillo, there's no time to explain it to you now, go away, go away... who sent you? Come on! Spill it out!...

CAMILLO: ... Mr. Carini...

ELENA: He's the father, idiot!... And he wants to keep the kid just to make me marry him! Wake up, idiot!

CAMILLO: ... What's so bad about that?... It seems like a good way to save face...

ELENA: What have I got to save?... Carini came in here and he fell in love with this house and everything that comes with it: he has every right to better himself, but not at my expense.

SCENE 101/A

Malvezzi House: Outside. Day.

Carlo awaits Camillo, who comes out without looking at him.

CARLO: Well, what did she say? How did it go?

Camillo walks faster, without answering, and breaks into a run around the corner.

SCENE 101/B

Church: Cloister. Outside. Afternoon.

Father Pino is playing "soldier's slap" with some boys in the cloister.

FATHER PINO: Was it you?

FIRST BOY: No.

Another slap.

FATHER PINO: Was it you?

BOYS: No, no, no!

Father Pino sees Carlo arriving.

FATHER PINO: Carlo, at last you've come back to us!

CARLO: Hi, listen, there's not a minute to lose...

SCENE 102
Dr. Valla's office: Landing. Inside. Afternoon.

Carlo and Father Pino race breathlessly up the stairs and arrive at Dr. Valla's office. Carlo rings.

CARLO: What'll you do?

FATHER PINO: God will show me...

CARLO: ... Hasn't he showed you yet?

SCENE 103
Dr. Valla's office: Examination room. Inside. Afternoon.

Elena has been put to sleep on the examining table.

The anesthetist checks her pulse.

The doctor pulls on his gloves.

NURSE: ... He's early.

DOCTOR: Tell him to come back in half-an-hour...

The nurse goes to the door.

NURSE: Who is it?...

CARLO: I've come to pick up the young lady...

NURSE *(behind the door):* The doctor says to come back in half-an-hour.

CARLO: What?

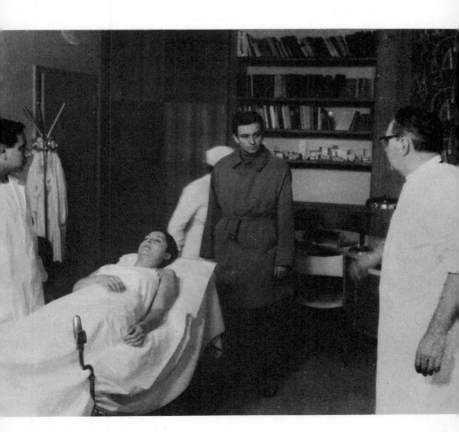

NURSE: Come back...

The nurse opens the door slightly. Carlo pushes his way in, followed by Father Pino.

NURSE: Just a minute! Pardon me, but where are you going? Doctor!

A heavy silence in the examining room: the embarrassment, fear and inexperience of everyone present in a situation of this sort.

In imitation of Christ, Father Pino throws himself on his knees, exclaiming:

FATHER PINO: Father, forgive them for they know not what they do...

The priest's action unfreezes the situation.

The doctor and the anesthetist consult feverishly together.

DOCTOR: Put away the instruments.

The nurse speedily collects the instruments.

Elena continues to sleep.

Father Pino's passion continues with an invocation.

FATHER PINO: O Lord Jesus love's light, I'm a sinner in Thy sight...

Carlo interrogates the nurse.

CARLO: Have you already done it or not? Talk! Are you deaf?

NURSE: No, no...

Carlo breathes a sigh of relief. Father Pino rises; his face alit, overcome by emotion, he stammers incomprehensible sounds. The doctor and the anesthetist come up to him with heads bowed.

DOCTOR *(to the anesthetist):* Watch what you say.

DOCTOR: Your appearance, Father, has been my Damascus...

FATHER PINO: Let us thank the Lord...

DOCTOR: ... Father, I would like to confess myself.

ANESTHETIST: I too, Reverend Father... for everything.

CARLO (to the nurse): Aren't you going to confess?...

NURSE: I haven't got anything to lose...

DOCTOR: Your pardon, Father, has been a revelation for me... so much that I would like to demonstrate my eternal gratitude to you with an offer for your parish...

Elena begins to move slowly.

CARLO (to Father Pino): ... Listen, Elena's waking up; I don't want to stay any longer... I'll talk to her later... Try to calm her down, you always find the right words...

FATHER PINO: In the meantime pray for her...

CARLO: Of course... (To the doctor) Doctor, I'd like to have a word with you...

Carlo goes off into a corner with the doctor.

DOCTOR: What is it?

CARLO: Be careful what you do, because I don't believe in this clowning like the Father does... Your professional future doesn't interest me, but if anything happens to Miss Gordini I will send you to jail even if you're not involved yourself at all... Do you understand? and another thing: give me back the money she gave you.

DOCTOR: ... But I don't have it on me...

CARLO: Then give me a check.

The doctor signs a check without batting an eyelash.

Elena opens her eyes.

Father Pino is beside her and waits for her to regain consciousness.

Carlo has gone out.

NURSE: What do we do now?

ANESTHETIST: We do what the priest says.

NURSE: Yes, but I want my pay.

SCENE 104
Astor Movie Theater. Outside. Afternoon.

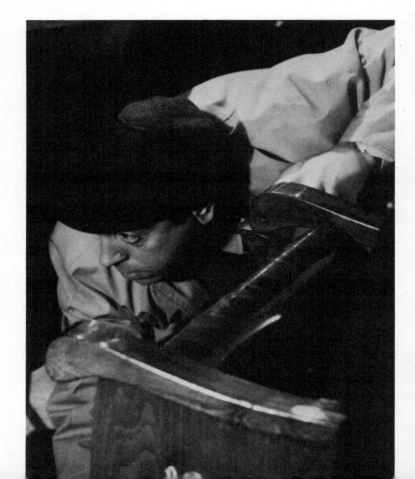

Vittorio is downtown with his two guns; the taxi has let him out at a movie theater.

Vittorio enters.

CASHIER: Orchestra?

VITTORIO: Orchestra, yes. Listen, can I leave these two guns here?

CASHIER: Yes.

VITTORIO: Thanks.

CASHIER: You're welcome.

SCENE 105

Astor Movie Theater. Inside. Evening.

Intermission. The house lights go on.

Vittorio calls over the snack-vendor.

VITTORIO: Have you got any peanuts?

BOY: Yes.

VITTORIO: Give me a package.

BOY: A hundred lire. Thanks.

Vittorio sits down and begins to open the package when he sees Camillo sitting a few rows ahead of him.

The theater is almost empty; Camillo need only turn his head to see his brother.

Camillo calls the boy over.

CAMILLO: Listen, give me a package of peanuts.

BOY: A hundred lire.

Vittorio cannot stand it; he rises, and as he moves rapidly along the row he does not notice that one seat has been left down; he bumps into it and falls.

Camillo recognizes him a moment before Vittorio falls below eye level, but he does not move.

Vittorio stays low until the house darkens, then leaves.

SCENE 106
Malvezzi House: Library. Red parlor. Entrance. Inside. Evening.

Giovanna is typing in the library as Carlo dictates.

CARLO: Cesare Ceccarini, Piero Zion, Carla Marzari... she won't have killed herself, will she?...

GIOVANNA: Sure, to spite you...

CARLO: Adamo Lerici, Giorgio Franconi, Annibale Lucci, Giuseppe Frabboni...

Vittorio enters the house; he comes to the studio with an upset expression; from his talk and walk he appears drunk.

VITTORIO: Good evening... What're you doing?

CARLO: Counting up the preference votes...

VITTORIO: You haven't seen Elena by any chance...

CARLO and GIOVANNA: No.

VITTORIO: And she hasn't called?... no message...

GIOVANNA: No.

VITTORIO: Can I have dinner?

GIOVANNA: Yes, it's ready.

VITTORIO: But I'm not hungry; will you keep me company?...

CARLO: Delighted.

SCENE 107
Malvezzi House: Dining room. Inside. Evening.

Enter Vittorio, Carlo and Giovanna.

VITTORIO: I just thought that when we count up the preferences, we have to count our two votes too... our three votes... did you remember?

CARLO: Yes, of course.

VITTORIO: I think it's legitimate that I vote for myself...

CARLO: Everyone does...

VITTORIO *(to Carlo)*: Sit down in my place, and put Giovanna there; I'm not going to eat; and Elena here, if she comes home... Did you read tonight's papers?...

CARLO: I glanced through...

VITTORIO: Any accidents?... scandals?...

CARLO: Nothing new...

Carlo and Giovanna sit at the table. Vittorio wanders about nervously. The telephone rings in the antechamber; Vittorio leaps for it.

GIOVANNA: He's drunk...

CARLO: Completely. Sit down, let's eat.

SCENE 108
Malvezzi House: Antechamber. Inside. Evening.

Vittorio at the telephone.

VITTORIO: Hello, is that you?

ELENA'S VOICE: You ran away, idiot. Why didn't you call me?

VITTORIO: Look, Elena, I did call you.

ELENA'S VOICE: No you didn't, I was home until six and you didn't call. Carlo terrified them all, the doctor begs me not to ruin him, the priest wants to redeem me.

VITTORIO: I called you...

ELENA'S VOICE: I'm finished, Vittorio, I'm finished, and all because you're an ass, an impotent, a good-for-nothing. Throw those two out of the house before I get home or I'll murder you.

SCENE 109
Malvezzi House: Dining room. Inside. Evening.

Vittorio returns to the dining room, dark and provocatory. Giovanna looks at the tablecloth and Carlo continues to eat. Without sitting down, Vittorio pours himself a glass of wine; he spears a piece of pie with a fork and gulps it down; he drinks the wine and takes a few steps about.

VITTORIO: Where are the car keys?...

CARLO: On the desk in the library...

VITTORIO: I should like to remind you, Mr. Carini, that when you use other people's property you're supposed to ask permission... It's an elementary rule of good behavior, in case you haven't been taught it... I think there are too many liberties being taken here with the employers' hospitality...

CARLO: Once, Professor, you told me I could take it whenever I needed it...

VITTORIO: Once, once... now I'm revoking this permission, or can't I perhaps? Did I commit myself in writing?... Another thing: everyone here has the door key... there's a doorbell that works perfectly well... so by tomorrow I want all the keys turned in...

CARLO: I'd advise you, Professor, to put a lock on the telephone too...

VITTORIO: Your wit is out of place here... And I take the liberty of suggesting, Mr. Carini, that at this point, a man with a minimum of self-respect would not continue to eat, as you are, off my plate...

CARLO: Perhaps you want to relieve me of my job too... Or this no, because you wouldn't know what to do next?...

VITTORIO: My dear Mr. Carini, whatever you say or do demonstrates your education... I relieve you of your job and you needn't worry about a recommendation; you'll have it...

Carlo walks out; Vittorio breathes a sigh of relief. He takes an enormous mouthful of pie.

VITTORIO: ... Giovanna, I realize that I have been attacked; like a bolt out of the blue, unfortunately, what is it, what isn't it; difficulties greater than ourselves have arisen: what are they? There's no point in talking about them; there they are, and even if we wanted to, we could never again return to that distance, that exclusively employer-employee relationship which we had before; I think the most reasonable thing is for us to separate, to separate, to separate... Naturally you will have excellent severance pay, greater than what I will give Carini, and you will always be able to count on this house any time you need protection, help or recommendations of any sort... more than this... if this is unjust, tell me; it seems just to me...

GIOVANNA: It's just, it's just, I'm not arguing. Only this speech would have been all right if you'd made it... even just a few weeks age...

VITTORIO: ... And why?

GIOVANNA: Because I think I'm pregnant...

VITTORIO: ... You think or you are...

GIOVANNA: I am...

Vittorio fills his mouth with another piece of pie.

SCENE 110

Malvezzi House: Outside. Night.

Elena and Furio are parked in his car; he has brought her back home.

ELENA: ... Well, will you marry me or won't you?...

FURIO: ... If you get rid of the kid...

ELENA: But if I get rid of the kid I won't marry you for the world!
I'd marry you because I've got the kid and can't get rid
of it!...

FURIO: If you want you can still do it...

ELENA: No, no: too many people already know I'm pregnant;
and then you don't know Carini...

FURIO: You should have told me first... a quick trip to Switzerland,
a weekend, and everything'd have been all right...

ELENA: All right, all right, I should have thought of it... but I
didn't... What do you care, Furio, if it's your kid or not!...
I assure you you'll never have to bother about him...

FURIO: Look, we live in a town of fifty thousand... people notice
right away if a kid doesn't look like its father; it's the first
thing they look for... if you want I can marry you after it's
born... a year or two later...

ELENA: ... All right, I understand, goodbye...

*Elena gets out of Furio's car, comes in the entrance-way and closes the door
behind her.*

SCENE 111

Malvezzi House: Stairway. Inside. Night.

Carlo, seated on the stairway, waits.

He hears Elena enter and hides.

Elena enters the house.

Carlo, reassured, leaves through the entrance-way.

SCENE 112
Malvezzi House: Library. Inside. Night.

Elena is raging. She sits down. The most absurd and revengeful ideas plunge through her mind. She sees several dozens of envelopes on her desk addressed to Vittorio's "Voters." She sweeps them to the floor, then rises, having reached a decision.

SCENE 113/A
Malvezzi House: Vittorio's bedroom. Inside. Night.

Elena enters Vittorio's bedroom without knocking; he is sleeping with Giovanna.

ELENA: Vittorio, Vittorio, hey, get up! Get up!

VITTORIO: What's the matter? Don't shout, are you crazy?

ELENA: I told you to get up; get up, obey me.

VITTORIO: Just a minute, here I come, here I come, let me put on my robe.

ELENA: Move, hurry up, get out, get out of here. *(To Giovanna)* In this house there's the masters' quarters and the servants' quarters; don't mix them up any more.

VITTORIO: Where are we going?

ELENA: Is this the way you threw them out?

VITTORIO: But I'm cold, I haven't got any socks on...

SCENE 113/B
Malvezzi House: Library. Inside. Night.

ELENA: Now I'll fix you all! You first. Here we've got to put a stop to this business instantly...

VITTORIO: Agreed, Elena, but couldn't we talk about it to-morrow?...

ELENA: During the day we can never speak: those two are always in our hair; anyway I'm not sleepy now...

VITTORIO: But I'm sleepy...

ELENA: I don't care!

Vittorio picks up the "Voters'" envelopes.

VITTORIO: But these are my preference votes! ˙

He finds one addressed to Elena among them.

VITTORIO: This is for you.

Elena puts the envelope on the typewriter table without looking at it.

ELENA: And then listen... are you going to stop sleeping with her or aren't you? Isn't one enough?... if you don't do it immediately I'll throw her out myself.

VITTORIO: Yes, yes, but give me a little time...

ELENA: There's no more time, there's no more time... anyway this isn't what I woke you up for: here we have to take inventory of everything in the house: right away...

VITTORIO: Are you mad?... and it's such a boring job too—endless. Just the sort of thing they could do...

ELENA: But it's for them I want to do it, idiot, and you want to have them do it themselves.

SCENE 114/A
City street. Outside. Night.

Carlo strolls down a deserted street of the city; he seems calm and euphoric. He stops to look at some posters with the enlarged picture of Vittorio, smiling, sure of himself, serene; a long row of them.

SCENE 114/B
Malvezzi House: Library. Inside. Night.

In the meanwhile Elena and Vittorio continue their absurd and pathetic inventory; they are exhausted and dishevelled. Vittorio, sitting on the floor, bounces a tennis ball as he continues to dictate one by one the titles of the books, which he reads on the bindings without removing them from the shelves.

VITTORIO: "Danger of Burial of the Dead..."

ELENA: Cut it out with that ball.

VITTORIO: "Life-Saving," "The Council of Pistoia," ten volumes, "History of China," "The Hopes of Italy," "Chemistry for Women"...

ELENA: Give it to me...

She takes the ball.

VITTORIO: Marcus Tullius Cicero, "Opera Omnia ad Usam Delphini," one, two, three, four...

Vittorio extracts a tall thick volume; he opens it. He begins to glance through it.

VITTORIO: The 1937 issues of "Victory"...

ELENA: Hey, are you sleeping?!...

VITTORIO: Let me rest a little...

Elena yawns and rubs her eyes.

As she collects the typed pages of the inventory, she notices the sealed envelope which Vittorio gave her; she reads the address: TO ELENA. She opens the envelope: it contains Dr. Valla's check, without any accompanying note. She is visibly pleased.

SCENE 115
Park. Outside. Day.

Vittorio bicycles in the park. An exercise to lose weight. Carlo drives by his side; the dog leans out the window into the breeze.

CARLO *(to the dog)*: Keep down, dopey... It's like talking to a dog... Here's the champ... *(To Vittorio)* Don't tire yourself out too much, Professor...

VITTORIO: Go on ahead, I'll meet you...

Carlo accelerates and immediately leaves Vittorio behind and then out of sight. It is a sunny autumn morning, the leaves have turned golden, etc. etc. Carlo has gotten out of the car and pulls the dog along on its leash (with some difficulty) towards an open-air bar which frames a dance-floor. The place is deserted; a juke-box is playing.

CARLO: Good morning.

WAITER: Good morning, Mr. Carini.

Carlo sits down on the bandstand.

The dog moves about; perhaps it wants more attention.

Carlo does not consent, and reproves it instead.

CARLO: Come on, calm down, take it easy. Learn to play by yourself. What d'you want? No, no, you won't get anywhere with me, you know. I'm not Camillo or Vittorio and you just leave me cold. You'll see how I'll make you run. I'm not going to be blackmailed by a dog. Go on, break your neck...

Carlo interrupts his sermon because Vittorio has ridden up. Vittorio greets the waiter, dismounts from the bicycle and sits down next to Carlo.

CARLO: Some workout, eh?

VITTORIO *(patting his stomach)*: All this has got to disappear. I really feel fine...

VITTORIO: ... There's no doubt that I took all the precautions to keep her out of trouble... agreed, the test confirms what she says... anyway, she wants to keep the child... Of course I feel affection for Giovanna, to say the very least, but I'm in a tight spot, very tight; do you get my meaning?... I'm about to become a public figure: this isn't the right time for marriage...

CARLO: Why should you have to marry her?... Who's forcing you? Giovanna is an adult and the law doesn't protect her any more... Professor, if you let me take care of it I'll settle the whole business.

VITTORIO: No, for the love of God... coming back to marriage, if this girl has to marry, since she does have to marry... there must be someone, not me, willing to marry her... you, with your great practical sense, Carini, I'm sure that if you think a moment about it...

CARLO: ... It's not so simple...

VITTORIO: You, for instance, could be an excellent husband for Giovanna... don't take offense... why not? You've both had the same education, you're both good workers, with the same problems... I've even learned that there was a little affair between you, a youthful sort of thing... so I think that with a little good will we can work out the appropriate conditions... And naturally, if you accept, besides being able to count on my unconditional assistance, you'd be able to have a couple of millions free and clear... and look, at this point I'd even give you the Department...

CARLO: It's too late.

VITTORIO: What? And why?

CARLO: Even if you wanted to, the Department would go to an elected Councilman...

VITTORIO: Come on, marry Giovanna... Look, I'm sure she's a woman who'll make her husband's fortune...

CARLO: Why not yours?...

VITTORIO: But it's different for me...

CARLO: Anyway... I'm already engaged.

VITTORIO: What?... You certainly don't think Elena will ever marry you!

CARLO: She confirmed it just this morning...

VITTORIO: Then what did you let me go on like that for?

SCENE 116
Philodramatic Theater. Inside. Noon.

The theater is filled to the brim; there are a few empty seats only in the last rows. Vittorio's speech will close his party's election campaign. The police force is nominally present in the person of two cops who are seated comfortably in one of the back rows reading comic books, which they exchange. The children, totally disinterested, run tirelessly all around the theater.

A heterogeneous audience; among the workmen, who are in the majority, stand out some elegant and haughty young people who have come simply out of curiosity, to see what Vittorio (still one of them) has become.

On the stage, behind the curtain, Vittorio, Carlo and several party officers.

CARLO: You've got the victory sewed up.

VITTORIO: Let me take a peek.

Vittorio looks out at the audience.

VITTORIO: Looks like there's a good crowd.

CARLO: You bet.

VITTORIO: Odd, there's not one empty seat. There must be three or four hundred people, eh?

CARLO: Look, shall we start? Then I'll announce. Stay calm, eh?

VITTORIO: Yes.

CARLO: Here we go.

As they talk, young Wolfgango passes by, carrying a basket; he walks toward the steps which lead below the stage.

Vittorio looks at him as if trying to place him.

With eyes lowered, Rospo enters the theater leading a German shepherd on a leash; he stops at the back of the theater and leans against the right corner.

CARLO *(announcing)*: Comrade Professor Vittorio Gordini.

Giacomo too enters with a German shepherd.

Camillo enters last of all, with a third German shepherd on a leash; he remains at the back of the theater, in the center, on the same line as Rospo and Giacomo. All three friends are at the ends of the now empty aisles leading to the stage. The audience is all seated. Each boy holds the head of his dog against his side so as to avoid attracting attention. One of the two policeman, tired of reading comic books, looks about and sees Camillo's dog a step away; he pets him for a moment and then looks elsewhere. Camillo ceaselessly caresses his own dog.

Vittorio is finally before the audience. He is alone, but seems unafraid. Applause breaks out at Vittorio's appearance.

VITTORIO: Friends and Comrades... we're on the eve of the local elections for our City and Provincial Councils: this is a matter which touches us at first hand, something of our

own, local, where the conflicts between Chinese and Russians or Chinese and Americans or French and Americans or Arabs and Israelis become temporarily secondary problems, because our local problems come to the fore: our unemployment, the municipalization of our pharmacies, the construction of new hospitals for us, of parks for our children, the end of our own housing crisis...

Applause.

Vittorio smiles as he waits for the applause to die down.

VITTORIO: ... So our voters must first of all come to know who the people are who are running for these offices, and they must have guarantees. I say this because my own candidacy has been the fixed target for almost the entire local press. The right wing accuses me of betraying my class, and the left wing of betraying the class I have chosen to represent. This situation now forces me to take this occasion to answer the most serious accusations levelled at me in the last few months. The most frequent of these is that I have changed political allegiance every season. Without ever having been truly a politician, I have sympathized with the Christian Democrats, the Social Democrats, the Communists, the Republicans and the Socialists... Apart from the imprudent but brief Communist parenthesis, interrupted disdainfully at the time of the Hungarian tragedy, I have supported each one of the four parties of the Center-Left coalition in turn. This open sort of political disposition (which by-the-bye is an experience common to many other Italians) is obviously not an index of moral fickleness, but the best guarantee that the Center-Left is not simply an emergency political coalition but an alliance which has been in the process of consolidation for a long period of time and has been predestined to take form; that is, that these four parties which make it up, even when they expressed contrasting political lines, were in reality already destined to converge,

because each of the four completes and is complemented by the other three, because what one repels the others accept, and vice-versa, because in at least one of the four there's a place for the Catholic or the laicist, for the young man or the old, for the poor man or for the rich.

That is, I believe that this quadruple alliance is a worthy representative of our Country; that is, it represents the majority of the Italian people...

Vittorio is surprised to observe the prompter's box slowly opening and then closing.

VITTORIO: My detractors have had the very poor taste to make clearly derogatory remarks even about my forthcoming wedding. Evidently they hoped to shame me and convince me to return to the ranks; but on the contrary they have obtained just the opposite result because I am one of those few idealists who still believe that a person can change, can be different from the way they were born, from the way they were brought up. To be more clear: in a provincial city it cannot be , denied that marriage is often considered as an economic deal.

Well what better proof that my hands are clean, than my forthcoming marriage? I'm marrying a Socialist! Yes, and I'm proud of it! I'm marrying a Socialist proletarian, one of yourselves. Is this not the best proof that I'm on the people's side? that I am a true democrat... I don't... that I am with you, on your side?... But there's a cat here!

In fact, the prompter's box has opened and Wolfgango has thrown the cat at Vittorio.

CARLO: Don't run, Vittorio, it's worse!

The two policemen pocket their comic books.

At the same moment Giacomo, Rospo and Camillo unleash the dogs, which race for the cat. The dogs leap onto the stage. The cat clings tenaciously to Vittorio's back; overcome with fear and roaring with pain, Vittorio flees into the wings without being able to shake off the cat. One of the German shepherds follows him; the audience shouts, laughs and stampedes out.

VITTORIO: Now I'll have to get a tetanus shot too.

SCENE 117
Malvezzi House: Gymnasium. Inside. Day.

Elena and Giovanna, in white smocks, are doing childbirth exercises out of the book "I'm Going to Be a Mother."

Giovanna is smiling and eager; Elena is unenthusiastic and resigned.

The End